PREACHER AS RISK TAKER

PREACHER
AS RISK TAKER

Richard Hart, O.F.M.CAP.

THE LITURGICAL PRESS
Collegeville, Minnesota

www.litpress.org

1   2   3   4   5   6   7   8   9

Library of Congress Cataloging-in-Publication Data
Hart, Richard, O.F.M. Cap.
    Preacher as risk taker / Richard Hart.
        p. cm.
    Includes bibliographical references.
    ISBN 0-8146-2147-3 (alk. paper)
    1. Preaching. I. Title.

BV4211.3.H37 2003
251—dc21

2002043348

To my mother,

Sylvia,

who continues to inspire me.

Contents

Introduction

Preacher as Risk Taker

Many individuals are risk takers. Mountain climbers, steeple jacks, Houdini magicians, bungee jumpers, farmers, and gamblers are but a few. But do we ever include preachers in that category? Very seldom, if ever. Yet preachers have the potential to be some of the greatest risk takers. This small book will outline how preachers can be on the cutting edge by taking risks, resulting in much better preaching.

How many preachers are willing to submit their homilies to an editor, like professional writers do? Excessive wordiness, some technical theological terms, and abstract phrases might need to be eliminated and replaced with crisp, concise words, phrases, and sentences.

Some preachers have found audio- or videotaping their homilies most helpful. What a powerful way to become a better preacher. Writers, golfers, musicians, and others are always looking for ways to improve their skills. Taping can be a humbling yet enlightening experience.

Every preacher is challenged to be a poet. Walter Brueggemann maintains that poetic speech is the only proclamation worthy of the name "preaching." A poet has great respect and feeling for the right words. Poetic preachers use exact and meaningful words that have the power of a two-edged sword.

Are we ready to preach in a changing church? We live in a pluralistic society and have multicultural listeners. Do we make the mistake of thinking we are preaching to people of strong faith or assume that everyone is Christian? How aware are we that the Church is in crisis comparable to the Reformation? Are we willing to preach on the critical issues?

One critical issue we need to preach on is sin, especially social sin, rather than the "mamby pamby" homilies on love. Have we ever preached on the environment? We often put this type of preaching in a subordinate clause because it is so difficult. Do we grasp that we are on a rapid course to ecological disaster or planetary suicide?

What becomes evident in the early Church is how Christians did not pray in order to preach and heal, but preached through healing. We can easily preach the doctrine of salvation without the salvation happening, or a doctrine of healing without believing that healing can happen. If all healing is spiritual healing and we are spirited preachers, we should be able to carry on the work of Jesus' healing ministry through our preaching.

We don't find many Gospel texts dealing with the call to grow old. On ageing we need to preach on what St. Paul stated, "Although our outer self is wasting away, our inner self is being renewed day by day" (2 Cor 4:16). How acquainted are we with the various aspects of ageing?

If we want to understand what the New Testament has to say about Jesus, we need to understand more clearly what wisdom (better known as *sophia*) is. Jesus "advanced [in] wisdom and age" (Luke 2:52). True wisdom is not a plethora of knowledge but the ability to understand, perceive, discern, and use good judgment. Jesus was truly a "wisdom figure" and needs to be preached as "the incarnation of Sophia."

What Jesus preached most was God's reign. Is this what we preach when the opportunity presents itself? Jesus proclaimed, "This is the time of fulfillment. The kingdom of God is at hand" (Mark 1:15). This was the inaugural of his preaching, the center and focus of his proclamation. Some describe him as obsessed with the vision of God's reign. God's reign, however, is not a concept but a person, the person of Jesus Christ.

We often shy away from preaching on the epistles of St. Paul and rather preach on the gospel or the first reading, because they are easier to preach and don't demand as much research and time. Another reason might be the way the Lectionary has been framed. Priority is given to the first reading and the gospel. Some of the passages from Paul are very brief and require a wider context that needs explanation. Often we need to read the whole letter or more sections of it to better understand and preach on the passage. Paul assures us, "How beautiful are the feet of those who bring [the] good news" (Rom 10:15).

Finally, how many of us really know the difference between a eulogy and a homily as stated in the Order of Christian Funerals? Again, it is much easier to preach a eulogy rather than a homily. Homilies need to be scripturally based. Often funeral homilies make little or no reference to the scriptural readings. Preachers have to show how the personal aspects of the deceased person are clearly connected with the scriptural texts. Finding the balance between scriptural proclamation and the person's lived experience is no easy task.

We might not be asked to scale a mountain, act as a steeple jack or Houdini magician, or fall like a bungee jumper. But preachers are asked to take similar risks when preaching on the above mentioned topics. Are we ready?

Chapter 1

Why Edit a Homily?

It is surprising and even a little shocking what a good editor can do to a rough article or manuscript. The editor might clarify the manuscript or article, eliminating repetition or excessive wordiness, despite the fact that the article or manuscript is considered practical, incisive, and of benefit to readers.

Imagine that every homilist had an editor comparable to a personal travel agent. Many of us would not be willing to undergo the editing of our homilies. Constructing a homily is challenging enough, especially adhering to a single goal, a single topic, being creative, relevant, and interesting. If the added requirement was to submit the homily to an editor, many of us would respond, "No way!"

Editing or revising a homily, however, is most important. Unfortunately, it is often omitted because of the time factor and hard work involved. Editing, we must remember, is done by professional writers. Hemingway cut out 100,000 words from *To Have and Have Not*. Newspapers, magazines, and movie or play scripts are also edited. Why not also for our profession, since we have such a powerful message to proclaim? Any homilists who want to be on the cutting edge need to edit their writing.

Few if any of us can claim that once we have written our homily it is a masterpiece which later will become a classic. Bishop Kenneth

Untener in *Preaching Better* states: "The primary purpose of writing in preparation for a homily is not to produce a great text; it is to think through a *thought* that will become a great homily and to work through ways of expressing and organizing this thought."[1] A good homily does not come cheaply or easily. If we are honest we will find extraneous material or words that need to be cut out. Maybe some technical theological terms crept in that are clear to us but not to our listeners. Abstract words need to be replaced with words that add color and substance to the homily.

An astute editor can set apart a homily so it is laced with concise words, phrases, and sentences. In the editing business there is a saying: "If you can't dance, you can't write." By this is meant that a good editor feels the cadence of language or the "musical beat" of words. We need to spend time editing but not to the point we become bleary-eyed. We will know when enough is enough. Words that are crisp, precise, and to the point are needed. The Gettysburg address consisted of 262 words. These words carved in the Lincoln Memorial still hold people spellbound because of their simplicity and depth. The Beatitudes proclaimed by Jesus are precise, crisp, and to the point.

What Needs Editing

Introductions often need editing. Good preachers arrange their material to grasp the listener's attention, thus inviting a response to God's Word. A brief but poignant story or a striking quotation might grasp their immediate attention. We have to make sure, however, that the introduction fits the main idea we are trying to convey. There are too many worn out introductions like, "In today's readings . . ." or "The Gospel today . . .," which immediately put our listeners to sleep, make them gnash their teeth, or click their off button.

We need to be certain that the homily contains only one main idea uniting the message. Some homilists are not satisfied unless they have touched on three scriptural readings. What often results is a two- or three-point homily that confuses the audience.

They mentally respond, "What is the preacher trying to say?" The preacher ends up talking to himself and not using the opportunity to drive home one idea. The same can be said of three subpoints in a homily, especially if they do not develop the main or central idea. Cutting will be in order. The main or unifying idea has to be repeated a number of times in the homily. Repetition helps clarity, coherence, and is an effective means to make the listeners aware of your principal idea. Jesus did this when he repeated the word "hypocrites" to the scribes and Pharisees. Repetition of the idea that God is love at the end of every paragraph can intensify the main idea. Dr. Martin Luther King Jr. did this well, as is demonstrated in *King Came Preaching.*[2] In his sermon "No Room at the Inn," he repeats "No room" at least a dozen times, so the audience knows what his central or main idea is. But revising might be necessary if we don't vary how we repeat the central idea. We can't expect our listeners to be riveted to our homily the way Jesus held people spellbound. Listeners are often distracted by people around them, babies crying, children acting up, so we need to invite them back into the mainstream of the homily.

Our homilies might also need revising if they are not an integral part of the liturgy. At times homilies have little reference to the Scriptures just proclaimed or the liturgical action. A homily is not a talk or a break in the liturgy. Conclusions are not meant to be drawn out but be brief, clean, and crisp. Preachers might ask themselves, does God add anything to a sunrise? Does an effective lawyer know when not to ask any more questions? The effective homilist knows when to conclude and might even do so by asking a question. Additional material or clarification has to be deleted no matter how important it might seem to the preacher. Some homilists have multiple conclusions and the listeners are mentally screaming, "Stop!"

Recently a woman commented about her pastor's conclusion to a homily: "He could have stopped two minutes earlier with a perfect ending." One preacher started his homily by asking those in the audience who considered themselves Christians or Catholics to raise their hands. The majority of them did. Then he preached on "love your enemies, do good to those who hate you, bless those who curse you, pray for those who mistreat you" (Luke 6:27-28). At the end of his homily he asked how many then considered themselves Christians or Catholics. Not too many hands were raised. What a fitting conclusion. Good preachers meet the challenge of concluding their homilies with an idea that flows easily into the rest of the liturgy. Often our conclusions need editing.

Looking at the Whole and the Parts

If we are going to edit our homilies we need to look at them as a whole and then the parts. We know how the homily fits together but the listeners don't. Will the material hold the attention of our listeners? Is the material very specific or general and nebulous? Being specific will attract listeners' attention. Pleading with the audience to "love your neighbor" does not have the same effect as specifically telling them "be kind to your neighbor even if he or she snubs you."

Do we at times go off on a tangent or what is some times referred to as side bars, asides, footnotes, or rambling? Sidebars are effective in newspapers as useful information put along side a story. Footnotes are not in the text because they interrupt the flow of good ideas being presented. But sidebars in homilies need to be eliminated because they clutter or digress from the main idea. "That reminds me . . . " is often a digression or a sidebar. "As I said before . . . ," "I could go on and on . . . ," are side excursions which need to be eliminated. We might interject words like, "he was, if I may use the term, boorish"; "his life hung, so to speak, by a thread." As seminarians we used to count the number of times one of our professors used "as it were" during his homilies.

Did you ever notice how editors use short titles for sections of the writing? These sections are the parts that make up the whole and help link the homily. So often those parts are obvious to us but are not to our listeners. Do they flow easily from each other? The parts must reinforce the main or central idea we are attempting to convey. If they don't, no matter how good and interesting the material is, they are to be edited, revised, or even dropped. Any irrelevant or useless material needs to be excised. Hard as this might be at times, the pruning process will bear far more fruit. This is one reason why our second homily on weekends is usually better than the first.

Vague Words

"Your neighbor" is an example of a vague or general term. Why not speak of "the newcomer on your block" or "someone who is sick in your neighborhood"? "Society" is an all-encompassing word. Instead use "members of your Elk Club" or "members of the Knights of Columbus." "People who are poor" is vague. Why not "people of the parish who are in need of a food basket"? "Bad habits" is broad and vague. Instead discuss specifics, such as using drugs, overeating, and drinking to excess. When we have a tendency to preach on "the evils of our society," we might specify racism, sexism, alcoholism. "Serving the Church" is too broad. Instead invite people to be a lector, eucharistic minister, or visit the sick.

General or vague words like great, fabulous, wonderful, terrific, marvelous, and super are easier to use, but they are also bland and ineffectual. Jesus did not use general or vague words: the farmer went out to sow his seed; the shepherd went after his lost sheep; the woman scoured her house to find the lost coin. The parables about the wheat and the tares, the man with two sons, the workers in the vineyard, the ten virgins, and the unforgiving servant are specific examples that his listeners understood.

One priest commenting on the words of Jesus—if your eye is an occasion of sin pluck it out, if your hand is an occasion of sin cut it off—asked how Jesus would apply these words today. He suggested that Jesus would speak about pornographic material available on the Internet or video rentals in stores. Jesus would also address the social sins of racism, sexism, and sexual harassment. He might suggest you pluck out your eye when you view pornographic material, or cut off your hand when you write checks way below the minimum wage for migratory workers. This is strong language. But remember Jesus was not afraid to call the scribes and Pharisees hypocrites, whitewashed tombs, full of dead men's bones, and blind guides (Matthew 23). Can we be more specific or graphic than that?

We could write "flowers were blooming everywhere" or "pink pansies glowed over the whole prairie." Notice that Jesus did not tell us to look at the flowers in the field, but specifically directed our attention to the lilies, which neither toil nor spin. There definitely is a heightened effect proceeding from the general to the specific. General words or phrases need to be sharpened by carefully examining our first draft and using, where necessary, more concrete and specific expressions.

Expressions which are general in nature also have limited emotional appeal. They act as dead weight in the sentence. Notice the vast differences between the words "cold" and "frigid" or "raw," between "hot" and "fiery" or "sweltering." Compound words can also add freshness. In Shakespeare's *Tempest* we find "virgin knot," "sour-eyed," "honey-drops," "foot-licker."

In his book on preaching Bishop Untener gives a sampling of words that fit the "abstract" category:[3]

faith commitment	lived reality	concretize	strategize
empowerment	parameter	sensitize	conscienticize
faith journey	problematic	marginalize	prioritize
mutually	receptive	actualize	theologize
spirit-led	faith community	interiorize	spirit-filled

The challenge for any writer is to avoid trite (comes from the Latin *terrere,* rub out, wear out) words and clichés like, "the man or woman of the hour," "the irony of fate," "conspicuous by one's absence," "this vale of tears," "powers that be," "last but not least," and many more. Or do we use euphemisms, synonyms for common terms which allude to something unpleasant like, "misrepresenting the facts" instead of "lies"; "underprivileged" instead of "the poor"; "mortician" instead of "undertaker"; "intoxicated" instead of "drunk"? As one writer pointed out, we probably would not think of eating a first-class piece of dead cow, but we might relish filet mignon of the finest quality.

Avoid using homonyms, two words that are pronounced the same, such as reign and rain, bear and bare. Alliteration (the repetition of initial consonant sounds), in most instances, is better read than spoken.

Finding the Right Word

Editing becomes even more painful when we spend time searching for the right words, especially verbs that pack a punch. Under which circumstances would we get out of the way faster: when we see a red sports car mount the curb and come toward us, or when a red sports car hurdles the curb and roars toward us? "Come" (as well as walk, go, run) is one of those colorless, hazy words, whereas "roars" is a power word, specific, and sharp. "Roars" also has the added dimension of sound. Looking for a good image or images is another way to enhance our homilies. Fr. Joseph Manton did this in his sermon on "A Funeral Is a Sad Sight":

> If Death were only the blunt end of a dead-end Street; if Death were only the tiny black period at the end of the sentence of life, with no page to follow, then every grave would be no more than a king-sized ashtray, and every headstone a monument to futile despair. But Death is not just an end. It is also a beginning. Death is not a wall. Death is a door.[4]

We might write about people having a bad outlook on life. Would not the word "jaundiced" have more meaning for most listeners?

Good homilies pack the action into the sentence where it belongs, the verb. "She made a plea" is not effective because the action is distributed; "she pleaded" is more dynamic. Compare "the homilist spoke in a loud voice" to "the homilist's voice boomed through the church." The second example explodes. Words or language can be compared to a wardrobe. Individuals will often say, "What should I wear today or on this occasion?" We need to choose the right word which fits or best suits the meaning we intend. The search is comparable to the man seeking a hidden treasure. If we are pleased with something, are we captivated, charmed, delighted, fascinated, or gladdened? Which word will we choose? A word exists to match a thought or a feeling. We need to match that word as if it were a lost piece in a jigsaw puzzle. And that explains why editing is painstaking. Don't be afraid to consult a thesaurus.

Unnecessary Words

These are the words that subtract from our message. Words like "this" or "it"—"it is," "there is," at the beginning of a sentence. Homilists who use a moralistic approach will pepper their sentences with "let us," "we should," "we ought," "we must." Be aware of using noninclusive words like "he" or "men." Here are more examples:

Instead of:	Use:
there are many people who	many people
and yet	yet
one of the reasons why God does permit suffering	one reason God permits suffering
that is why we are tempted	when tempted
as we know from history	history tells us
we know from the life our Divine Savior	from Christ's life we know
among those people who are prosperous and evil	among prosperous and evil people
a quality he lacks is politeness	he lacks politeness
the thought comes over you	the idea dawned

Avoid the passive voice because the usage causes indefinite statements and wordiness. For example, "when the passive voice is shunned, a few words are very often saved," can be changed to "shunning the passive voice definitely saves a few words." The rule is that brevity demands the greatest number of ideas in the shortest space. Brevity can be as effective as the short spear used by the Roman legionary.

The various forms of the verb "to be" are often static. "There is the desert" could be enhanced by "there stretches the desert"; "here is the temple" to "here towers the temple." Gracefully avoid the static "is" where possible.

Editing means looking at your homily with a fresh pair of eyes. By lively injections of the right word or words, chiseling away at phrases and sentences, we polish the homily into what we hope will be a slam dunk! The time spent is not a waste because it adds sparkle and vigor to your homily. With the help of a computer we can cut, copy, paste, undo, redo, or put the homily into another file while keeping the original draft.

An editor of my book *Preaching: The Secret to Parish Revival,* wrote:

> I have yet to run into an excellent preacher who was also an excellent writer—and I have had the opportunity to work with a number of fine homilists. OK writers, yes, and plenty of good ideas to work with. Perhaps the two disciplines may be almost diametrically opposed: to be a good writer may mean enough rules and disciplines that spontaneity and such are sacrificed. I don't know; this would be an interesting debate, no? Maybe you are that homilist because you have practiced well both disciplines.[5]

Notes

[1] Bishop Kenneth Untener, *Preaching Better* (Mahwah, N.J.: Paulist Press, 1999) 61.

[2] Mervyn A. Warren, *King Came Preaching* (Downers Grove, Ill.: InterVarsity Press, 2001) 198–203.

[3] Untener, *Preaching Better,* 88.

[4] Joseph Manton, *The People and the Steeple* (Huntington, Ind.: Our Sunday Visitor Press, 1953) 12.

[5] Letter sent to me by Mary Carol Kendzia of Twenty-Third Publications, January 25, 2000.

Chapter 2

To Tape or Not to Tape

If it is true that very few topics elicit more opinions from parishioners than preaching (music is also up there on the list), preachers might be inspired to work on preparing and delivering their homilies more effectively. Preparing solid homilies each weekend can be most challenging, especially for busy ministers. A forceful way to prepare and deliver better homilies is to audio- or videotape them.

Bishop Kenneth Untener of Saginaw, Michigan, conducts a diocesan-wide program on preaching. He and a small group of priests, a deacon, and a lay preacher convene to evaluate their preaching efforts. Back in 1993, with the total support of his Presbyteral Council, Bishop Untener started a preaching program. A letter is sent to four priests, a deacon, or a lay preacher. In most instances this is done in alphabetical order. They are asked to tape a Sunday homily during the next three weeks and send it to the bishop. The amazing part is that this has become a requirement in the diocese. Bishop Untener also tapes one of his homilies and adds it to the others.

After receiving the homilies his secretary mails the participants a "kit" containing a tape and a typed manuscript of the homilies. (He comments that his secretary is going straight to heaven.) The participants listen to the homilies and take notes on what they observe. The group then gathers in his office for two hours to discuss the homilies. No professional homiletics professor is called in.

Other Evaluators

The director of communications is invited for part of the session. She is a veteran journalist who selects and edits two transcripts. These are circulated and she reviews and explains her corrections. The participants easily recognize the difference between written and spoken word, and the journalist readily acknowledges that. Her expertise is not theology or homiletics; she is a journalist who applies her skills to this task. For many priests this process is startling and appreciated.

Another person who is a systematic theologian and skilled spiritual director also participates. She offers insights "from the pews" because she is neither the homilist nor the liturgical minister. According to Bishop Untener both these women bring welcome insights to the group.

Additionally, someone in the neighboring diocese lines up a group of lay people who participate in the project by mail. After hearing the tape they offer their written comments, which frequently echo those made by the diocesan group.

The idea is to help each other become better proclaimers of the Word, much like other professions benefit from workshops or meetings. The evaluation or critique of each homily is very specific. The group insists on honesty. Bishop Untener reminds them of the importance of this task, which he believes is at the heart of their ministry. The ensuing conversations are lively and far ranging. They might discuss what a homily really is, the joys and sorrows involved in preaching, or what the parishioners are thirsting to hear proclaimed.

After two hours another date is set and the process is repeated. Each participant takes another blank tape to record a future homily. This is done four times. A letter is then sent by the bishop to four other priests, plus a deacon or lay preacher, and a similar process is begun.

Honing Our Skills

All of Bishop Untener's preachers have undergone this process. He believes that preachers—like authors, musicians, golfers, and other professionals—should continue to perfect their skills. After listening to over a thousand homilies and having his own critiqued, he readily admits how much he has learned. His book *Preaching Better* outlines what he has learned.

A number of years ago I replayed a student's audio recording. It was the first time he had heard himself on tape and he could not believe this was his voice. He was so dismayed by the sound of his voice that he ran out of the room. Upon hearing themselves on tape for the first time most individuals are surprised by or have a hard time accepting that is their voice. Experts tell us that cupping our ears forward will give us a better idea of our true sound. Radio broadcasters are sometimes seen doing this. Whatever we sound like, we cannot deny it or make excuses because tape recorders do not lie. They record only what is said.

Cleveland Diocese

A project similar to that in Saginaw is being conducted in the Cleveland diocese where they have set their priority on preaching. In October 2000 a one-day convocation on preaching was held. Two hundred seventy-five priests gathered and were challenged to make the most of an important opportunity to reach the area's one million church members. They learned that it is one thing to talk about spending more time preparing homilies, and another thing to follow through. Due to retirement and the death of many priests, and low numbers of candidates entering the priesthood, precious time is often devoted to aspects of the ministry other than preaching. An article in the Milwaukee Archdiocesan *Catholic Herald* reported that Fr. Ronald Bandle collapsed and died while celebrating Mass at St. Joseph parish in Lyons, Wisconsin. He was only fifty-six. Parishioners as well as clergy and friends were deeply shocked at his untimely death. The Milwaukee archdiocese had only one ordination in 2002, and he was a belated vocation.

The priests of the Cleveland diocese were encouraged to evaluate their schedules and make preaching a priority. Fr. Edward Estok Jr., administrative assistant and secretary to Bishop Anthony Pilla and director of continuing education and formation in the diocese, stated that the proclamation of the word is the primary call and responsibility of the ordained.

After the convocation of priests in November 2000, centering on "The Priesthood and the New Evangelization," they enrolled some eighty priests in a ministry entitled "Priests' Preaching Support Ministry." Their earnest hope was to build fraternity in their role as preachers as well as address the problem of preaching. Borrowed from industry, the "coaching" method was wholeheartedly adopted at the convocation.

They ran a pilot-round before the convocation and surveyed the twenty-three participants to find out the challenges and successes. The priests were given the option of video- or audiotaping their homilies. The group unanimously endorsed videotaping over audiotaping. Most of the priests verified that seeing and hearing themselves on tape proved most beneficial for them.

Father Estok is also involved in preaching instruction of their diocesan seminarians. The first theologians take a course entitled "Proclamation and Oral Interpretation." The faculty employ the coaching method in all five preaching courses or labs available throughout their students' formation process. Father Estok is convinced that videotaping makes all the difference in helping others to preach better.

For a period of three months priests who were involved in this project have taped one of their homilies and received feedback from their parishioners. Then they meet with the purpose of discussing ways to improve the homilies. A very effective method for doing this is knowing what you want to say and sticking to one idea. The priests agreed that one of the biggest traps of all preachers is multiple points.

Walter Burghardt, S.J., in his "Preaching: Twenty-Five Tips," offers a suggestion for testing your next homily: "(1) Fashion a text; put on paper what you want to say, as completely as possible,

(2) Arrange for an audio tape of the homily as actually delivered, (3) Compare the two versions."[1]

Videotaping

Reverend Guerric DeBona, O.S.B., homiletics teacher at St. Meinrad School of Theology, feels very strongly that videotaping is far superior to audio recording. In his "Introduction to Homiletics" class, he and a student view the student's homily tape individually. (The students are required to produce a text, but they do not have to use it to preach.) With both written and performance guides to shape his course, he finds that students have learned more from visual observance of the videotape. After all, he argues, this is what the Christian assembly will see along with those unspoken gestures and facial expressions. Father DeBona maintains that it is both a comforting and sobering experience to witness oneself in the act of preaching. Much can be learned from the act of seeing.

Fr. James Wallace, C.SS.R., and Fr. Robert Waznak, S.S., who teach courses in Preaching I and II at the Washington Theological Union, videotape all the student homilies. Father Wallace suggests, however, that the students view the tapes a number of ways: the first-reaction viewing; then a viewing done with the sound off with the students watching for body language, facial expressions, and gestures; next a "hearing" of the tape, turning away from the screen and attentively listening to what the voice is doing; finally, a full viewing to see if anything else strikes them. Father Wallace believes there is value in simply listening to a homily since preachers can focus on what their voices are doing—intonation, cadence, emphasis, and changes in affect.

Father Waznak prefers videotaping because it demonstrates the whole person in communicating the Gospel. He does, however, insist on some caveats. More important than the instrument are the affirmation and challenges offered by the mentor who uses the instrument (audio or video). Video can sometimes be tricky. Students might focus on the fact that they have gained weight or lost hair rather than how they are presenting their message. Father Waznak believes a student should not view the tape immediately but let some time pass. It might be more beneficial to view it after a few days, a week, or even a month to gain a better perspective.

Fr. Stephen De Leers, homiletics instructor at St. Francis De Sales School of Theology in Milwaukee, Wisconsin, states that they do not have the latest equipment for videotaping. The seminarians go out to various parishes to preach and are responsible for any videotaping that is done. He realizes that he is in the minority, but he favors audiotaping where good interaction can result from playing back the tape.

A Valuable Tool

Sr. Joan Delaplane, O.P., who teaches homiletics at Aquinas Institute of Theology in St. Louis, has found videotaping a valuable and positive tool during her twenty-three years of teaching. She tapes her students but admits she has not made it a practice to watch the tapes with them. This is her dream because she believes watching the tapes would be very helpful. Occasionally she does ask a student to meet with her to watch the tape. Students are scheduled to preach seven times in the Foundation Course and in the Liturgical Preaching Course. In the Advanced Preaching Course they preach about four times. At the end of each she asks the students to review the videos of their preaching events, evaluate their progress, and determine what needs to be addressed. She feels that the students are fairly accurate in their assessments or appraisals. Sister Joan finds that watching the video is a positive experience for the students, especially when they see their nervousness is not as obvious as they thought.

At St. John's Seminary in Camarillo, California, Fr. Daniel E. Harris, C.M., videotapes every homily given by his students. He considers this an essential part of their growth. He meets with each student after class to carefully review the tape. The student can see what Father Harris is talking about when he refers to specific issues in the student's preaching.

He follows a different strategy when his interns tape homilies in parishes. The videotapes they have submitted in the past usually have very poor audio, since the camera was positioned a significant distance from the preacher. Father Harris now asks the interns to place an audio recorder on the pulpit or connect it directly to the parish sound system.

Father Harris maintains that videotapes offer a fuller experience of the preaching event. He uses a video camera that is connected to the parish sound system or equipped with a wireless microphone, although he realizes that many parishes are not able to supply this level of technology.

Critiquing Videotapes

Fr. Andre Papineau, S.D.S., who teaches homiletics at Sacred Heart School of Theology in Hales Corners, Wisconsin, appreciates the value of audiotaping homilies. However, he is convinced that videotaping is far more effective if done on a regular basis. He videotapes about twenty students, then asks them to review the tapes and critique themselves. Videotaping, according to Father Papineau, more effectively reveals the nonverbal communication and visual cues given by the homilist. It is one thing to tell students about distracting mannerisms such as dancing around, lack of eye contact, stilted gestures, but when they actually see these things on tape they cannot deny them.

Father Papineau believes that peer feedback is also important. He recommends that after students finish critiquing their initial sermon, they videotape the homily a second time, implementing the suggestions to see the improvement. He also admits that he doesn't have the time to critique all the videos.

Some years ago I videotaped one of our friars preaching a homily in a Milwaukee parish. I also turned the video camera on the audience and invited anyone to stay after the Mass when we reviewed the tape. A number of them did and were surprised how they looked during the homily. The friar found this recording most helpful and, undoubtedly, this first experience helped him become the fine preacher he is today.

There is little doubt that audiotaping homilies can prove most helpful in improving our preaching. But an even better approach is to videotape the homilies, as many of the homiletics professors have pointed out. The benefits far outweigh the obstacles. Improving our preaching is not a matter of simply taping the homilies. Rather, we need to accept the challenge, no matter how good we are or think we are, because the experience can be a humbling yet enriching way to preach powerfully and forcefully the Good News.

Note

[1] Walter J. Burghardt, "Preaching: Twenty-Five Tips," *Church* (Winter 1996) 20–3.

Chapter 3

Preacher as Poet

The title of this chapter sounds like alliteration and has a certain pizzazz about it. But for a preacher to be a poet is indeed risky and challenging. Both poets and preachers can move or inspire others by what they say or write. Poets have the ability, as Ezra Pound wrote, to express their "poetic thought works by suggestion, crowding maximum meaning into the single phrase, pregnant, charged, and luminous from within."[1] The question arises, does our preaching do the same?

In *Finally Comes the Poet,* Walter Brueggemann states:

> By poetry, I do not mean rhyme, rhythm, or meter, but language that moves like Bob Gibson's fast ball, that jumps at the right moment, that breaks open old worlds with surprise, abrasion, and pace. Poetic speech is the only proclamation worth doing in a situation of reductionism, the only proclamation, I submit, that is worthy of the name preaching. Such preaching is not moral instruction or problem solving or doctrinal clarification. It is not good advice, nor is it romantic caressing, nor is it a soothing good humor.[2]

Coleridge maintained that poetry was the best thoughts put into the best words. Good preaching is the same. Preachers need to have a feeling for the right words, a respect for their value or worth, as well as their limitations. Words have their individuality. T. S. Eliot brought this out when he wrote:

> . . . where every word is at home,
> Taking its place to support the others,
> The word neither diffident nor ostentatious,
> An easy commerce with the old and the new,
> The common word exact without vulgarity,
> The formal word precise but not pedantic,
> The complete consort dancing together.[3]

Preachers, however, can make words their slaves or masters. This can be true especially of description where it can become a master instead of a servant. Words are neither slaves nor masters, but are our friends. Jesus said to his apostles at the Last Supper, "I no longer call you slaves, because a slave does not know what his master is doing. I have called you friends, because I have told you everything I have heard from my Father" (John 15:15).

What really matters is what the poet or preacher has to say. Good poetry as well as good preaching reveal the subject matter but conceal much of the poet or the preacher. Their experiences are manifested by means of their words and images. Often these words or images fall short of their fullest meaning. But the preacher, like the poet, must continue to study the words and images. This discipline results in a spontaneity like David dancing before the Lord. Just as David was moved to dance, so the preacher and poet unite with God's creative activity to say what needs to be said. Without a poet's approach to life, a preacher's language will often not be precise. Unless we speak poetically about God's love for us, we will never be able to articulate that love properly to our listeners.

Jesus' Sermon on the Mount is definitely precise and economizes words. Some have described it as a perfect sermon and a perfect poem. It certainly gives a graphic description of the qualities necessary for discipleship, and is the Magna Carta of Christianity. If we want to find out what kind of Christians we are, the beatitudes offer a powerful blueprint or perfect model. They teach us about righteousness and our capacity for new life.

Importance of Words

Homilies as well as poems depend on words. But if we examine their words, they often don't reveal their secret lives. Most preachers are not known for their skill with words. What a preacher does while not preaching gives meaning and life to the preaching. At times we proclaim something, and later ask, did I say that? Those moments might be rare for some preachers, but the deeper one's faith, hope, and love, the more frequent they become. Then the words of Isaiah will be true:

> All of you kindle flames
> > and carry about you fiery darts;
> Walk by the light of your own fire
> > and by the flares you have burnt! (50:11).

Words are often weak, old, tired, faded, and worn thin by daily use. In *Better Preaching,* Bishop Ken Untener gives a list of twenty abstract words, twenty-one overused words, and thirteen overworked phrases.[4] But words can be musical, help visualize images, solid as the strongest steel, repetitive like an enchanting dance making the preacher mute when he speaks them. Often we don't understand the words but only their fury. Words have the power of a two-edged sword, but they also can be a tinkling cymbal and a sounding brass, or in common parlance, a blaring loudspeaker piercing to the ears. But God still remains God even in the weakness or lack of luster of human words.

Every true poet speaks words from the heart. So also the true preacher. A true preacher does not point to one's own heart but to the heart of Jesus saying, *Ecce Homo!* There is always an innate danger that a preacher may become pretentious, even narcissistic, drowning himself in his own importance. But even if the Word of God does not come from the heart, God is not limited by the preacher. Isaiah assures us:

> For just as from the heavens
> > the rain and snow come down
> And do not return there
> > till they have watered the earth,

> making it fertile and fruitful,
> Giving seed to him who sows
> > and bread to him who eats,
> So shall my word be
> > that goes forth from my mouth;
> It shall not return to me void,
> > but shall do my will,
> > achieving the end for which I sent it (55:10-11).

God's Word accomplishes its aim.

Primordial Words

If it is true that primordial *(Urworte)* words are entrusted to the poet, the Word of God is also entrusted to the preacher. The poet and the preacher speak the primordial words with utmost concentration and beauty. Good preachers convey the primordial Word of God, a Word of mercy, forgiveness, compassion, and love. In this sense the preacher is always a poet, maybe not an ideal one, but God's poet for others. Primordial words richly express the meaning of life and how life is worth living. Poets speak primordial words in powerful ways, and preachers are invited to do the same.

Take the word "water" as spoken by a chemist or by St. Francis of Assisi. Francis referred to it as "sister water" and the chemist as H_2O. This primordial word when used by a chemist is reduced to a technical word. According to Goethe water is our very soul and one can't substitute H_2O for that. One word is not as good as another. Primordial words often cannot be defined. If we attempt to do this, we "kill" them. People can write and have written oceans of words, but when distilled all one might have is a jug of stale water. Primordial words will endure the test of time, words like love, star, flower, spirit, sorrow, time, and eternity. By trying to explain these primordial words we cheapen them. Everyone speaks primordial words but not the way the poet and preacher do who pronounce primordial words with freshness and vigor. A poet is sometimes referred to as the minister of the primordial sacrament of words. How much more the preacher!

Choosing the Exact Words

Words can be a preacher's crucifixion when we need to fashion the correct or exact words to convey a precise meaning. Words are powerful or powerless, bland or full of life, clichéd or packed with meaning, abstract or concrete, boring or moving listeners to action. Words have power to divide as well as unite, to explain the parts of the whole, to make others confused as well as illumined, to obscure as well as enlighten. Forceful words will always come at a high cost or with an expensive price tag. Finding the right word can be a thorn in the flesh for some preachers. Even though words are expressed vividly by poets and preachers, ultimately they are God's gift to others.

The task of poets and preachers is to become weavers of exact and meaningful words. Walter Burghardt, s.j., maintains that

> two words, "Seig Heil" bloodied the face of Europe; three words "Here I stand," divided the body of Christendom. Words have made slaves and freed slaves, have declared war and imposed peace. Words sentence to death ("You shall be hanged by the neck") and words restore to life ("Your sins are forgiven you").[5]

Rosemary Haughton writes that poetry remains the most forceful and accurate way to communicate the incommunicable. Poets have the innate skill to name the nameless, to comprehend the complexities of life.

Poetry in Scripture

Are not the first beginnings of the world and humanity sheer poetry? The state of innocence is marred by sin's origin. The book of Job contains much poetry. The psalms are filled with majestic poetry. So many passages of Isaiah contain profound poetic expressions of God's love and concern for humanity. Only a poetic prophet could speak of God's love or self-giving in terms of endearment, but often at the price of his own blood. That was certainly true of Jeremiah. He gives us poetic glimpses of new life in chapters 30–33. The prophets pointed out the absence and presence of God; they were poets entrusted with God's Word which spoke a powerful message to the people. And the greatest prophet of all spoke in parables. Don't most people feel the beautiful poetry found in the parable of the prodigal son? The tears of remorse certainly fell on the shoulders of the prodigal father. Jesus' priestly prayer found in chapter seventeen of St. John is poetic. One can feel the rhythmic poetry of John's Gospel, "In the beginning was the Word, and Word was with God, and the Word was God" (1:1). St. Paul's description of love in 1 Corinthians 13 is truly a hymn of glorious poetry, as was the hymn in Philippians 2.

Preacher's Experience

I. A. Richards wrote, "Communication takes place when one mind so acts upon its environment that another mind is influenced, and in that other mind an experience occurs which is like the experience in the first mind, and is caused in part by that experience."[6] Preachers need to ask, what is the experience of the first mind? Wordsworth described poetry as emotion recollected in tranquility. Can this describe our preaching? Even when preachers or poets attempt to recall the experience, this becomes a new or fresh experience. That implies that every good homily or poem is never a reproduction. Recently a man who attended both Masses that I celebrated told me that the homily at my second Mass was better than the first one. I remember developing it differently.

Even if a preacher repeats a homily fully written out it is still not the same. Preachers change between the two homilies, and certainly the listeners are not the same. Most of us are aware of this as we preach. But are we fully aware of the subtle effects on us and how we deliver the Good News? Besides, sometimes the test of a good homily is not how much the listeners remember, but rather what effect it had on them. Are there the same old quarrels on the way home or at the dinner table? Are listeners still impatient, irritable, and crabby when things don't go their way? Does the homily move them to social action?

Artist

R. G. Collingwood describes an artist or poet in these words: "The artist must prophecy not in the same sense that he foretells things to come, but in the sense that he tells his audience, at the risk of their displeasure, the secrets of their own hearts."[7] Isn't this true of a preacher? No community knows its own heart, and can often deceive itself just as Adam and Eve were deceived. Or a community will turn a deaf ear to the message and have recourse to something less threatening. God's Word does accuse and abuse as well as comfort. The Good News is the best medicine for any disease of the mind. Good preaching confronts a community like the prophets did. Be truthful and that truth will make it free. Hans Urs von Balthasar wrote concerning prophets, "God needs prophets in order to make himself known, and all prophets are necessarily artistic: What a prophet has to say can never be said in prose."[8] Preachers are often reduced to silence when speaking in prose, but not in poetry.

An artist and a preacher must move from their ivory towers to help build up a Christian community, one able to face the challenge of change and confusion. Perhaps congregations are often bored and unresponsive to our homilies because we are not artists practiced at our craft. Poetry helps the preacher to know and appreciate the hallmarks of true art. Preaching becomes an art when it broadens the experience of the community. A difference exists between the mechanics and the art of preaching. Mechanics are the structure of the homily, the use of imagery and imagination, illustrations, persuasion, humor, and storytelling. Art is the ability to engage listeners at the level of their daily existence. Preaching is both a religious and artistic act that draws people together. So we don't need to be a Newman, John Donne, Bossuet, Lacordaire, or a Bishop Sheen. We need to be artists at work who love our form of art.

The true artist brings excitement and freshness to one's work, captivating our minds and hearts by keeping our attention. The same should be true of preachers, otherwise our listeners will be bored and ready to leave. Art is at the very core of our preaching, bringing preacher and community closer together.

Jessica Powers is such an artist, showing how she is a citizen of love and also God's ambassador:

> Having no gift of strategy or arms,
> no secret weapon and no walled defense,
> I shall become a citizen of love,
> that little nation with the bloodstained sod
> where even the slain have power, the only country
> that sends forth an ambassador to God.
>
> Renouncing self and crying out to evil
> to end its wars, I seek a land that lies
> all unprotected like a sleeping child;
> nor is my journey reckless and unwise.
> Who doubts that love has an effective weapon
> may meet with a surprise.[9]

Poetic Vision

Frederick Buechner, a famous Presbyterian minister, had poetic insight in his sermon on "The Road to Emmaus." He proclaimed that we can never nail down Jesus even if the nails were real like the ones on the cross. Jesus suddenly and unexpectedly appears out of nowhere like lightning or a sudden thunderstorm. We might recognize him or we might not. But our lives will never be the same after we have encountered him like the disciples on the way to Emmaus. Maybe Thomas Aquinas received that kind of poetic vision or insight when he realized that all his writings were like straw.

One way to obtain a deeper poetic vision is to read poetry or become more acquainted with various forms of art. Burghardt reads poetry like Shakespeare, Hopkins, T. S. Eliot, and E. E. Cummings before setting pen to paper in preparing his homilies. He claims this turns on his creativity and the homily won't sound like a laundry list or a Roman rescript. No wonder he likes the words of Rod McKuen:

> I make words for people I've not met,
> those who will not turn to follow after me.

> It is for me a kind of loving,
> A kind of loving, for me.[10]

The more we read and acquaint ourselves with poets, the more we might be ready to quote them. If our homily pertains to God's creation we might quote some of Gerard Manly Hopkins' poem:

> The world is charged with the grandeur of God.
> It will flame out, like shining from shook foil;
> It gathers to a greatness, like the ooze of oil crushed.
> Why do men then now not reck his rod?[11]

If we preach on Mary we might also resonate with Gerard Manley Hopkins:

> If I have understood,
> She holds high motherhood
> Towards all our ghostly good
> And plays in grace her part
> About man's beating heart,
> Laying, like air's fine flood,
> The deathdance in his blood;
> Yet no part but what will
> Be Christ our Saviour still.[12]

Karl Rahner asserts that priests should be poets. Preachers are challenged to be masters of imagination and left-handed thinkers as poets are. That entails being master storytellers, using imaginative parables, employing vivid imagery so evident in Jesus' preaching.

A Capuchin brother of mine, Alexis Luzi, concluded his homily on St. Francis of Assisi in the context of the parable of the vineyard in this way:

> When you go in hot pursuit of the beggar [i.e., the poor], when you bend down to kiss and embrace a leper, or when you start talking to the birds or your cat or your dog, you are not only not in your right mind, you are also a *poet*. So Oscar Wilde says that "Francis had the body of a beggar but the soul of a poet." Now being a poet might not be a big deal for some people, especially for

those solidly right-handed thinkers in our midst. But it is the poets and the Francises ("those great lefties"), who in every age, are the powerful Left Hand of God, marvelously and melodiously restoring the vineyard of the Lord.[13]

Walt Whitman expresses well what the poet and preacher struggle with:

> After the seas are all cross'd,
> (as they seem already crossed,)
> After the great captains and engineers have
> accomplish'd their work,
> After the noble inventors, after the scientists,
> the chemist, the geologist, ethnologist,
> Finally shall come the poet worthy of that name,
> The true son of God shall come singing his songs.[14]

Yes, after all this, finally comes the preacher-poet. Will it be you?

Notes

[1] Ezra Pound, letters quoted by Herbert Read, *The True Voice of Feeling: Studies in English Romantic Poetry* (London: Faber & Faber, 1953) 23.

[2] Walter J. Brueggemann, *Finally Comes the Poet* (Minneapolis: Fortress Press, 1989) 3.

[3] T. S. Eliot, *Four Quartets* (London: Faber & Faber, 1944) 42–3.

[4] Bishop Kenneth Untener, *Preaching Better* (Mahwah, N.J.: Paulist Press, 1999) 88–90.

[5] Walter Burghardt, *Preaching: The Art and Craft* (Mahwah, N.J.: Paulist Press, 1987) 6.

[6] I. A. Richards, *Principles of Literary Criticism* (London: K. Paul, Trench, Trubner, 1938) 177.

[7] R. G. Collingwood, *The Principles of Art* (Oxford: Oxford University Press, 1938) 336.

[8] Hans Urs von Balthasar, "The Glory of the Lord," *A Theological Aesthetics* (New York: Crossroad, 1982) 43.

[9] Robert Morneau, *Poetry as Prayer: Jessica Powers* (Boston: Pauline Books and Media, 2000) 61–2.

[10] Rod McKuen, *Listen to the Warm* (London: Michael Joseph, 1968) 112.

[11] *Poems and Prose of Gerard Manley Hopkins,* selected by W. H. Gardner (Baltimore: Penguin Books Inc., 1953) 27.

[12] Gerard Manley Hopkins, "The Blessed Virgin Compared to the Air We Breathe," *The Poems of Gerard Manley Hopkins,* ed. W. H. Gardner and N. H. MacKenzie (London: Oxford University Press, 1957) 93–7.

[13] Homily given by Alexis Luzi on the feast of St. Francis, October 4, 1999.

[14] Walt Whitman, "Passage to India," 5:101–5, *Leaves of Grass* (New York: Mentor Books, 1954) 324.

Chapter 4

Preaching in a Changing Church

Most of us will agree while living in the second millennium that the assemblies to which we preach are different than twenty or thirty years ago. Many denominations complain that their people have little background in their Christian faith. We preach today to multicultural listeners living in a pluralistic society, which can present a problem to some preachers and a risk or challenge to others. Which do we choose? Maybe the basic problem, according to Peter Ochs, is "that the burden of our age is not too much faith and too much church, but a condition of broken relationships."[1] This leads to individualism, which is rather rampant in our society. Faith and reason end up competing rather than complementing each other.

Some listeners don't really know God but desire to meet God. Some do not believe in Jesus Christ, but have heard about him and are curious. Or perhaps they have heard about Jesus and want to know more about him. Preachers need to respond to inquisitive and at times suspicious people. One of the big mistakes often made is taking it for granted that we are preaching to people of strong faith. Years ago people could recite answers from the Baltimore Catechism. For example, a sacrament is an outward sign instituted by Christ to give grace. How many today are acquainted with the new catechism unless they have taken a course or attended an RCIA program? If we use terms like the Synoptic Gospels, Pentateuch, paschal mystery, eschatology, or hypostatic union, how many will understand us?

Loren Mead's book *The Once and Future Church* maintains that we need to question our assumptions. No longer can we assume that "everybody is a Christian." How many of our listeners, as well as ourselves, are living the Gospel values? His suggestion is that we return to the apostolic age, when the front door of the Church was always open to mission territory. We might argue that we have always been a mission Church, but how vigorously have we pursued this goal? Our identity as a Church is intimately connected with our mission.

The Good News will always be what Jesus has done for us, his willingness to go up to Jerusalem to suffer, die, and rise. Our task is to preach that message in fresh and invigorating ways. We need to offer to our listeners a better way to live which ensures a hope-filled future in a world often mired in cynicism. So many of the saints offer concrete examples of courage, generosity, and the highest kind of love because they believed in Jesus' death and resurrection. Their belief was so deep and profound that many of them were willing to risk their own lives to demonstrate their convictions. Their mission is as old as the Dead Sea Scrolls and as fresh as a new born day.

According to Franz Cardinal Konig, perhaps for the first time the Church has become a universal Church. That means that everyone is invited and should belong, not just certain people, groups, or nationalities. He remembers how at one time in his life it was important to defend one's faith against other religions. Now the question has changed to what is implied or meant for an African, Italian, European to live one's religion or faith.

The Church in Decline?

We often hear of the large number of people no longer attending church. This is true of other denominations as well, not just limited to Catholics. Rabbi Heschel explains that attendance at religious services has declined not because it was refuted, but rather because many people find religion irrelevant, insipid, and oppressive. When one's faith is completely replaced by one's creed, worship by laws, love for a group of habits, we have a real crisis. Rabbi Heschel maintains that when our faith becomes a fountain of new life not a heirloom of the past, that when we speak out of compassion and not rigid authority, then the message will be meaningful instead of meaningless.

Bishop Kenneth Untener maintains that membership in the Catholic Church has increased, but participation in Sunday Mass has declined. These people, however, still consider themselves members, as is evident at Christmas and Easter. Years ago we had two choices: go to Mass or go to hell. Now people don't believe that. We preached a message of fear rather than Jesus' message of love, compassion, forgiveness, and mercy.

Crisis in the Church

We are well aware of how the Church is in crisis. The wrangling and debating often reach fever pitch. Archbishop Rembert Weakland, O.S.B., once observed that many parishes have become debating societies and gossip mills. Strong opinions do not mean we are a divided Church. Most families exemplify this division. The media often gives this impression because of the biased lens through which present issues are viewed. The list of critical issues is well rehearsed: sexual abuse by priests, inclusive language, homosexuality, abortion, the ordination of women, closing or uniting parishes, the international debt, global warming, immigration, divorce, and remarriage. Are these and similar issues symptoms of something deeper? Some experts believe it is fear. As preachers we need to address these changes and fears because they have cosmic proportions. Maybe we need to ask questions like: What does it mean today to be human, a people of faith, a Christian living in a pluralistic society? How do we live amid our differences of opinion? How do we learn more about the different cultures in our midst as Bishop Nicholas DiMarzio has emphasized? Do we address the changes in the ethic makeup of parishes?

Are we aware or convinced that the shortage of priests has helped the lay ministry to blossom so quickly? With the closing of some parishes the old axiom is still true, "For something to have been good, it doesn't have to continue." Parishes are closing not just because of diminishing numbers but also due to population shifts.

We can counteract the crisis by encouraging others to live their faith and celebrating it to the fullest. We need to replace crisis with celebration. The council documents insist that the summit and source of our Christian worship is the Mass. We need to probe more deeply the place of art, music, dance, and preaching in the liturgy—what Andrew Greeley calls the "apologetics of beauty." In the Mass we come together to praise and thank God for all we have received and continue to receive. There we are nourished by the Word (the importance of a good homily is crucial) and sacrament. Then we are sent forth to live the Good News and bring it to others. Some of the most consoling words of Jesus are found at the very end of Matthew's Gospel, "Behold, I am with you always, until the end of the age" (28:20). We need not fear crisis, for as the psalmist says:

> God is our refuge and our strength,
>> an ever-present help in distress.
> Thus we do not fear, though the earth be shaken
>> and the mountains quake to the depths of the sea,
> Though its waters rage and foam
>> and mountains totter at its surging.
> The LORD of hosts is with us,
>> our stronghold is the God of Jacob (46:1-4).

Matthew's Gospel

It is possible for us to preach Matthew 16:19 where Jesus said to Peter, "I will give you the keys to the kingdom of heaven. Whatever you bind on earth shall be bound in heaven; and whatever you loose on earth shall be loosed in heaven." But listeners often do not grasp the fullness of reconciliation which is proclaimed by Jesus in Matthew 18:15, "If your brother sins [against you], go and tell him his fault between you and him alone. If he listens to you,

you have won over your brother." So it is possible to confess a sin of rudeness but continue to be rude. Definitely something is missing and there is the need to reconcile with the other person. Matthew 18:16 stresses the need to resolve the situation and to even go further: "If he does not listen, take one or two others along with you, so that 'every fact may be established on the testimony of two or three witnesses.'" If the first encounter fails, we should seek the advice of a wise person. There is strength in numbers. The book of Deuteronomy states, "One witness alone shall not take the stand against a man in regard to any crime or any offense of which he may be guilty; a judicial fact shall be established only on the testimony of two or three witnesses" (19:15).

If this approach fails, according to Matthew's Gospel, we should take the matter to the fellowship of Christians where the case may be judged in a spirit of love and prayer. Should all this not produce any results, then we might regard the stubborn person no better than a tax collector or a Gentile. But even that person can be forgiven as was obvious from the lives of Zacheus and Matthew. So we don't ever abandon the individual as hopeless but continue to love the person because as St. Paul tells us, "Love never fails" (1 Cor 13:8).

The problem with some liturgists is that they construct their reconciliation rituals around Matthew 16 rather than Matthew 18. Imagine what would happen if we had rituals designed where husbands and wives could ritualize their forgiveness, or children doing the same, as well as local churches.

Speak Out Against Abuses

Imagine also what would happen if we spoke out more vigorously against our materialistic and consumerist society, the global injustices, and human rights abuses. An example is what has happened to Iraqi children as a consequence of our embargo. What would happen if we took more seriously visiting the sick, the home bound, prisoners, orphanages? These people are falling into safety nets, which are being dismantled knot by knot. Martin

Luther spoke of the Church as an infirmary for the sick. Why can't we speak of the Church as a hospital?

A healing, caring Church would help to counteract the anxiety or concern for ourselves and our personal needs. Certainly this entails an uphill struggle comparable to salmon swimming upstream. But we need to encourage our listeners to be a welcoming Church to the outcasts and those considered impure in our society. Preachers need to challenge listeners to live with the insecurity and ambiguity this entails.

Shifted Emphasis

Our previous emphasis was on a hierarchical church, but since Vatican II we have shifted the emphasis to a pneumatic and charismatic people of God. We preachers need to heed the words of the Ephesians: "the whole body, joined and held together by every supporting ligament, with the proper functioning of each part, brings about the body's growth and builds itself up in love" (4:16). The concept of ministry needs to be broadened so that all are looked upon as channels of God's grace. In *The Shape of the Church to Come,* Karl Rahner has stated that the gifts of God's presence in the Church can serve to "shock" the institutional life of the Church which can act "solely as the doctrinaire guardian and teacher of abstract principles which become ever increasingly abstract and are liable to carry within themselves the danger of a terrifying sterility."[2]

We have to make sure that some gifts are not marginalized, that we don't value one gift over another, or believe that the Spirit is limited in granting gifts. Pope John Paul II in his encyclical *Donum et vivificantem* insists that whatever is done with Gospel values is an example of the Holy Spirit at work. Preachers should make listeners more aware of their gifts, and that they are the salt of the earth, the light of the world. Experts point out to us that using 20 percent of our brain potential is extraordinary. Anthropologists maintain that we use about 10 percent of our brain power, which means there is a lot of untapped potential in everyone.

By enhancing and encouraging the use of their gifts, they will become more conscious and aware how they are "wounded healers" applying the balm of Gilead to others (Jer 8:22; 46:11; 51:8).

We also need to motivate our listeners to an active interest in what is happening outside their own church doors. Before Vatican II "outreach and social concerns" were not as evident in most parishes as they are now. These areas might include sponsoring hot meals served to the homeless, a headstart program, visiting a nearby prison, working with Habitat for Humanity. Too many people are like Dives in the Lazarus story. We dress ourselves in rich purple and bypass Lazarus, who is waiting for the crumbs to fall from our table. It is important to remember that many inner-city parishes differ from wealthy suburban parishes. Inner-city parishes often offer clothes for the poor, food pantries, health clinics, and support groups. It is inspiring to see how some suburban parishes help these parishes, especially with offering hot meals.

Keeping Abreast of Topics

Preachers are challenged to keep abreast of current topics such as welfare reform, *Roe v. Wade,* the death penalty, racial issues, HIV/AIDS, gay and lesbian people, the international debt, and other thorny issues. How many of us even broach the subject of AIDS, especially when we know that some people think it is God's plague on people who have sinned? Joseph Cardinal Bernardin wrote:

> The Gospel reveals that while Jesus did not hesitate to proclaim a radical ethic of life grounded in the promise of God's kingdom, he never ceased to reach out to the lowly, to the outcasts, of his time— even if they did not live up to the full demands of his teaching.[3]

Maybe cradling an HIV-positive baby in our arms might change our preaching.

Racial issues not only divide our nation but they also divide and trouble our Church. Is it still true, as someone has claimed, that the most segregated hour in America takes place at 11:00 on

Sunday morning? The Church must not be a bastion of racial exclusivity. Are we carrying on the tradition of the Samaritan woman at the well—"For Jews use nothing in common with the Samaritans" (John 4:9)? We need to alert our listeners to anything that perpetuates exclusivity. We have to equip them, as Marvin McMickle writes, with skills "to live in a multi-cultural society where Rhamadan and Passover are as accepted as Christmas and Easter."[4] When we sing "God Bless America" that does not mean we believe that God doesn't bless other countries as well, or prefers our country to some other. The book of Genesis does not state, "In the beginning God created the United States of America." A true missionary thrust spreads the Gospel message of justice, love, and equality to all people, no matter where they live. Then these values can be lived more fully in their daily lives.

We also need to ask if we are condemning the refugee crisis in Africa with the same urgency as found in Europe or elsewhere. Are we condemning the genocide of blacks in Liberia as vehemently as the genocide in Kosovo or Serbia? Martin Luther King Jr. expressed it well when speaking about the Vietnam War that any injustice done anywhere is truly a threat to justice everywhere.

Evangelization

Walter Burghardt, S.J., quoted Pope Paul VI's document *Evangelization in the Modern World*: "Evangelization cannot be complete unless account is taken of the links between the gospel and the concrete life of men and women. The Church considers it highly important to establish structures which are more human, more just, more respectful of the right of the person, less oppressive and coercive" (29 and 36). He believes that a quarter century later,

> all too many Christian preachers either do not believe it, or believing it, are reluctant or afraid to preach it. The consequence? Encouragement without challenge; biblical sermons bereft of the prophets; a bloodless Jesus who never said, "Blessed are those who are persecuted for justice sake" (Matt 5:10). Ultimately, just a church, a cordial fellowship of believers, not a just church.[5]

He maintains that we have to go beyond ethical justice to biblical justice, which implies fidelity to our relationships with God, others, and all of creation. Jesus preached right relationships. People like the paralytic, the woman at the well, lepers, Zacheus, and others were restored to the human family. Like Jesus we need to challenge people to love strangers, foreigners, immigrants, people we dislike, enemies, and even terrorists.

Are we preaching in Wal-Mart churches where you receive a basket or cart rather than a warm welcome and a bulletin? "Hang out" places today are not churches but shopping malls, especially for teenagers. Yet churches should be offering warm hospitality where people are not badgered to buy, buy, buy, and pay later. Does our preaching help us become a Wal-Mart community or a "cloud of witnesses" as found in the book of Hebrews (12:1)?

Robert Barron, systematic theology teacher at Mundelein Seminary, believes that if we are anchored in Christ and have a sense of mission, we can gather material from any source which is available to us and then mount any pulpit to proclaim the good news. We need not be hampered by any culture (God is much greater than any culture). Rather, we are challenged to be creative and undaunted in choosing from various sources like Aristotle, Einstein, Chesterton, and Cicero. Dr. Martin Luther King Jr. was accused of having recourse to many non-Christian sources in his sermons. He certainly was a modern day prophet. Are we willing to preach a prophetic message?

Over sixteen centuries ago St. Augustine was convinced that people were looking at the Church saying that it was going to disappear, die. "Christians will be no more" was the drumbeat. But even as they pronounced the death knell to the Church, the Church continued to live on. We are challenged to preach in a changing Church that will live on. Are we willing?

Notes

[1] Peter Ochs, "Church and Sociality," *Living Pulpit* (October–December 2000) 4.

[2] Frank Macchia, "Rediscovering the Church's Charismatic Structure," *Living Pulpit* (October–December 2000) 29.

[3] Walter Burghardt, "Just a Church or a Just Church?" *Living Pulpit* (October–December 2000) 11.

[4] Marvin A. McMickle, "Preaching That Challenges Our Understanding of the Church," *Living Pulpit* (October–December 2000) 39.

[5] Burghardt, "Just a Church or a Just Church?" 10.

Chapter 5

Dare We Preach on Sin?

William R. Burrows, managing editor of Orbis Books, maintains that

> preaching on sin is perhaps the most difficult thing a pastor can do. On the left side of the church are those who seethe, muttering under their breath, "What's he trying to do, bring back all that guilt I had such a hard time getting rid of in therapy?" On the right side, they sit waiting for condemnations of the loose standard's of today's church and muttering afterwards, "See, he just doesn't have the guts to name sin."[1]

Many preachers, as well as people, have a natural aversion for the topic. Some revel in the fire and brimstone approach. It is certainly not necessary to make our listeners wallow in their guilt or cause a guilt trip. Guilt is usually already present if people have spurned God's love. Sin instills guilt and shame in most listeners, so preachers prefer to talk about love, compassion, forgiveness, and mercy. One preacher decided to talk about sin during Lent, a good time to approach the subject. But when the parishioners found out ahead of time they asked, "Are you actually going to preach about sin?" So the title was changed to the "S" word. Although sin is not a favorite topic among most parishioners, a few months ago I preached on sin because the Scriptures dealt with the theme. After Mass one of the ladies said to me, "I am glad you spoke on that subject, we hear too many mamby-pamby homilies on love." As preachers we have to ask ourselves, do we become anxious when we preach on the topic of sin? Or are we eager to seize the opportunity and take the risk?

Brian Pierce, O.P., states that "preaching is really the oral art of truth-telling. It is the process in which the preacher seeks to form words around central gospel truths in a way that they are grasped anew as liberating Good News by communities of faith."[2] Jesus insisted that "the truth will set you free" (John 8:32). One of the powerful ways to set free people chained by sin is to preach the truth about sin.

Jesus talked about sin only a few times as recorded in the Gospels. He said, "I did not come to call the righteous but sinners" (Matt 9:16). Paul, however, refers to sin at least sixty times, forty-eight times in Romans. We read in John's first epistle, "If we say, 'We are without sin,' we deceive ourselves, and the truth is not in us" (1 John 1:8). The Old Testament depicts sin as a revolt against God. Søren Kierkegaard, in *Either/Or*, preferred men and women of the Old Testament because they knew how to sin. The rest of us, he lamented, lack the moral vitality to be sinful. Remember the definition some of us learned about sin as "an offense against God." In the New Testament the "offense against God" is worse because now we have God's most precious gift of Jesus. To sin also means a repudiation of the love of God, who sent his only son to suffer and die for us and bring us new life.

Sin

Sin is far more sinister than knowing that stealing or cheating is wrong. Sin means to miss the mark, to wander off the road, the inability to hit the target, the lack of a destination. Sin is a perversion of humanity. Sin frustrates God's purpose of making us in God's image and likeness. If all people were born to reflect God's image, then we need to stress how inhuman people can be toward each other by selfishness, not caring and loving, not being generous, being unjustly angry and violent. That is the sin—our inhumanity toward each other. Jesus exemplifies what humanity should be. Jesus was aware that no one was so perverse as to completely erase God's image. Too many Christians view life as avoiding big sins or observing proper manners. Preachers need to challenge listeners to become more Christ-like. That entails living more deeply in God's presence, having an awe and reverence for all creation like St. Francis of Assisi. Preachers need to show that the Christian life might more accurately be defined not just in doing virtuous acts, but through a deeper awareness of God's presence everywhere, which is then reflected in the daily lives of believers. True Christians are challenged to see more deeply, to listen more actively, and to speak more kindly wherever they are. Sin blinds listeners, helps them to put their hands over their ears as the people did when Stephen spoke, and enables them to spread gossip, detraction, and calumny. With David we need to say, "I have sinned against the LORD" (2 Sam 12:13). It is good that God "has not dealt with us as our sins merit, / nor requited us as our deeds deserve" (Ps 103:10).

Sin is often described as a separation from God. The opposite is also true that Jesus who was sinless shows us how it is possible to draw closer to God. Sin is basically a violation of freedom which is compromised by guilt. When we fell out of Eden we did not fall into our own Catholic Church. We fell into the jaws of temptation and the swamp of evil. Just as God put a mark of approval on Cain, so also God has put that mark on us. But sin is as sneaky as the serpent tempting Eve. It is a virus infecting individuals and a whole world. We are shackled by individual and social sin and can become its slave. But we are free to choose between good and evil. No individual is forced to sin. The wages of sin are not only death but also ironic. We sin because we are human beings, we misread much of reality, we so often listen to our fears rather than our hopes.

David Knight in his book *Living God's Word* asks:

> What has changed? For one thing, the Church recognizes that theologians were too quick to agree on what actions were serious enough to be "mortal sin." To miss Mass one Sunday would send

you to hell as surely as committing murder would. And since missing Mass was a more common temptation than murder, priests preached on it more. The result was that Catholics were more concerned about missing Mass than they were, for example, about whom they killed in war. By declaring so many things "mortal sin," teachers made us less able to recognize real evil when we saw it.[3]

Do We Trivialize Evil?

One way to trivialize evil is to be concerned about personal sin only, rather than social, systemic, or structural sin like racism, sexism, violence, corrupt multinational corporations, and oppression. By making sin exclusively personal preachers have a tendency to trivialize evil. Evil becomes manageable when listeners are told they can straighten out their own lives. In many ways the devil is left off the hook and preachers can lessen listeners' need for God. Preachers need to point out how listeners have to struggle with the powers and principalities of the world.

What also occurs is that we shift the blame for all the evil in the world on someone or something else. We point fingers at others where once our arms embraced. As long as evil is elsewhere it holds people together. It did for the Germans, the Japanese, and the Russians.

Now that Catholics don't have Protestants or some other group to hate (except in Ireland) we have each other. Carl Jung insisted that all unconscious negative material will be projected on someone else. In Leviticus 16 we read about the scapegoat which was spat upon, received a crown of thorns and the sins of the people, and then was sent out in the desert. Do we realize who was the greatest scapegoat? Jesus! We are the only religion that worships a scapegoat. The virus of sin was taken away by Jesus on the Cross.

Social Sin

Evils like the Holocaust and ethnic cleansing do not make sense when understood in personalistic terms. Some experts who consider the Holocaust one of the worst sins ever committed have boldly maintained that we human beings have lost or are in the process of losing our humanity. What motivates the behavior of those in power to perform such dastardly deeds is more important. It is rather fruitless to blame others for rampant racism or oppression. A deeper analysis of the causes of these evils becomes most challenging for the preacher. And is it not amazing that despite our marvelous advances in technology we still feel so powerless in preventing evil?

Is the decline in the sacrament of reconciliation due to the fact that people are sinning less? Is there any evidence to substantiate this? I doubt it. One of the main reasons sin is so sinister is that many people have lost their sense of sin. We are disturbed by the shootings in West Padukah, Kentucky, Jonesboro, Arkansas, and Littleton, Colorado, and the snipers, John Allen Muhammed and Lee Malvo. But do we see ourselves as part of the problem or understand how real sin is? Possessing a sense of sin means facing the reality that we are born into a sinful world. The murders, rapes, and atrocities of Kosovo, the hatred between Catholics and Protestants in Ireland, the hostility between the Palestinians and Israelis, the persecution in Sudan are just a few of the painful reminders.

Other examples are the entertainment industry, which often has as its goal nothing but pure violence of human beings. Nintendo games teach participants that violence is not unlawful but actually fun. How ironic! Or consider the sexual and domestic abuse, the hate groups like neo-Nazis, the adultery which often comes to light, the racism running rampant in many areas. Few people realize that they are racists, and many do not have that intention. But people are born into racism, and the more we try to sweep it under the rug the more racism raises its ugly head. With the advent of television, I can remember whenever my Dad saw a black person appear on the screen, he would immediately turn the channel. One time he and my mother visited me at a parish where there were a number of black people attending Mass. He immediately said to my mother, "Let's get out of here." Racism is a sin as the bishops in their pastoral letter have pointed out very forcefully. Archbishop Rembert Weakland insisted on the need to challenge racist attitudes by preaching repeatedly that all people are created equal. He also insisted that preachers are responsible for the attitudes of most people. We need to preach on this topic over and over again, clarifying how all of us are created according to God's image. If we don't, he maintained, we don't belong in the preaching business.

Consider the bombing of the Federal Building in Oklahoma City or the World Trade Towers in New York City. The hate crime committed against Matthew Shepard which left him to die chained to a fence post. The "skin heads" who dragged a black man behind their pickup. Our inhumanity at "work." We need to alert listeners to recognize the dark side of humanity.

Change of Heart

Preachers have to help listeners to change their hearts, attitudes, or mind sets. Even though our listeners will never be fully healed or changed, we can encourage them to change their lives by letting go of their sinful attitudes. We need to proclaim that change is possible and that is the good news. If one person changes, others are bound to be affected. To better understand how this is true, especially in the area of social sin, preacher and novelist Frederick Buechner compared humanity to a giant spider web. If you touch it anywhere the whole web is set in motion. Using images to describe sin or evil, irrational concepts that don't make sense, is a powerful method. Evil or sin ought not fit into a pattern. Often the only way we can preach about sin is by means of images, symbols, and stories.

We sometimes hear our listeners say, "What can I do? I am only one person, like a piece of sand on the whole seashore of life." They need to realize the effect of speaking a kind word rather than a harsh or sharp word, or a favor done for someone rather than an excuse of no time. By reaching out and touching someone in a loving, caring way maybe that person will do the same for someone else. The opposite is also true.

Mother Theresa counteracted the evil and sin she saw in the streets of Calcutta by picking up human beings who were left to die, and look at the impact she had. Terrible as the Holocaust was it also brought out much goodness. One Jewish survivor told how he and his brothers were hidden by a Polish Catholic woman. She was willing to expose her whole family to imminent danger. He declared that he could never do what she did. He might have been able to face danger himself, but not risk the lives of his children. Indeed, she was no ordinary person but extraordinary, perhaps even a saint for what she was willing to do. She restored his faith in God.

Paul's Struggle

St. Paul depicts sin as a person wanting to do good but actually doing evil (Rom 7:19). So often our good intentions are contradicted by our actions. Virtues can turn into vices. This applies not only to individuals but to communities, families, churches, and nations. Father Sava, a Serbian Orthodox priest of Decani, Kosovo, criticized President Milosevic but also told the *New York Times* that the NATO bombing had disastrous effects: the good intended ended in a humanitarian disaster. (Could the same be said about our bombing Afghanistan?) He warned former Secretary of State Albright what would happen to the Kosovo Albanians if NATO started bombing. Former president Clinton flew to Guatemala to apologize for the active role the United States played in their bloody civil war. But have any significant actions or policy changes followed from this long-overdue apology?

Once St. Paul points out how grace reigns more than sin, he asks the question, "Shall we persist in sin that grace may abound? Of course not! . . . You too must think of yourselves as [being] dead to sin and living for God in Christ Jesus" (Rom 6:1, 11). This needs to be preached, especially that we live more fully God's presence in Christ Jesus.

Differences Between Men and Women

Feminist theologian Valerie Saiving suggests there are differences between men and women regarding sin:

The temptations of woman as woman, are not the same as the temptations of man as man, and the specifically feminine forms of sin—"feminine" not because they are confined to women or because women are incapable of sinning in other ways but because they are outgrowths of the basic feminine character structure— have a quality which can never be encompassed by such terms as "pride" and "will to power." They are better suggested by such terms as triviality, distractibility, and diffuseness; lack of an organizing center or focus; dependence on others for one's own self-definition . . . in short, underdevelopment or negation of the self.[4]

Masculine and feminine sin are not opposites because of gender. People are not programmed to sin a certain way, but develop their own pattern of sinning independently. Man's sin of "will to power" perpetuates woman's "under development or negation of self." And it is also true vice versa.

How Do We Prepare a Homily?

When planning a homily it is important to talk to people about sin. We will find that a teenager's sense of sin is much different than someone who is seventy or eighty years young. Is a man's definition or attitude toward sin any different than a woman's? Attempt running the word "sin" through your website search engine to see what is available. Are there any recent articles or books on the topic? Anne Lamott in her book *Traveling Mercies* writes that people are not punished for their sin but by it. Do we agree with that? Is it safe to say that sin has its own punishment? Sin is really an act of self-violation and destruction altering one's personality. While stressing the seriousness of sin we must preach how God is "merciful and gracious . . . , slow to anger, abounding in kindness" (Ps 103:8).

There are close to eighty references on sin, the fall, and original sin in the Catechism of the Catholic Church. Concordance searching is always a fascinating adventure. Are there movies (like *The Mission* or *Amistad*) or plays which have depicted sin well?

Wrestling with the question, "From where does sin come?" is always challenging. Augustine's classic definitions of sin—any desire, word, or action contrary to God's law, in addition to turning away from God and toward a creature—certainly are disputed among theologians today. What are theologians saying about sin? Why is corporate or social sin a more difficult subject on which to preach? Are we afraid to step on people's toes when we preach on that kind of sin?

As preachers we need to remember that we are not sinless or virginally pure. Do we practice what we preach? When was the last time we loved someone we disliked or maybe even hated? Like Zacheus we need to come down off our sycamore tree and accept Jesus' invitation to dine with him where he extends his friendship to us. In imitation of Jesus we have to "deal patiently with the ignorant and erring," because we also are "beset by weakness" (Heb 5:2).

There are two cities, the City of Sin and the City of God. In the City of Sin people miss the mark, wander off the road, and lack a destination. They show their inhumanity toward each other through racism, sexism, violence, oppression, and then shift the blame to something or someone else. In the City of God people follow in the footsteps of Jesus by becoming more human. That means they are more compassionate, loving, caring, forgiving, and they practice social justice. There the ministry of Mother Theresa and the Polish Catholic woman is carried on, building up the reign of God. Dare we preach on sin? We better if the City of God is to be built up into a new Jerusalem.

Notes

[1] William R. Burrows, "Seeing Sin's Deepest Perversion," *Living Pulpit* (October–December 1999) 10.

[2] Brian Pierce, "Sin and Telling the Truth," *Living Pulpit* (October–December 1999) 30.

[3] David Knight, *Living In God's Presence* (Cincinnati: St. Anthony Messenger, 1999) 51.

[4] Patricia R. Case, "Talking about Sin, One Expert to Another," *Living Pulpit* (October–December 1999) 20.

Chapter 6

Have We Ever Preached
on the Environment?

When was the last time you preached on the environment or mentioned it in a homily? Many of us have shunned this topic mainly because it presents a difficult challenge and risk, or we are not convinced of its importance. Many of us put this type of preaching in a subordinate clause or have a poor track record on this vital issue.

We live on an earth of over six billion people where a delicate balance exists between animal and plant species as well as natural resources. Many experts believe we are on a rapid course to ecological disaster or planetary suicide. Competent biologists like E. O. Wilson, Norman Myers, and Peter Raven claim that this is the worse devastation done to our earth since the end of Mesozoic period over 65 million years ago. We are not aware of how many plant and animal species disappear every day, and maybe forever. Some biologists maintain that twenty thousand plant and animal species are becoming extinct every year. That would amount to one species every thirty minutes because of polluting the air, water, soil, and the raping of our forests. Each one of these species represents a unique face of God, and each is important for the proper functioning of our planet which took billions of years to evolve. We terminate them forever without batting an eyelash. Why? Is it because we can live more comfortably and enjoy a convenient lifestyle? Pope John Paul II has said that our society will not find a solution to our ecological problem until we look seriously at our lifestyle.

In a 1991 pastoral letter the Catholic bishops of Florida stated that

> Catholic teaching has long cautioned against life styles that place material goods and consumption ahead of spiritual values and ethical relationships. The pursuit of self-gratification on an excessive level places a burden on our individual lives and relationships, on our natural resources, and on our environment. It is especially important that we evaluate our consumptive habits and reorient ourselves to more frugal, nurturing and caring lifestyles.[1]

For people who desire to simplify their lives, Cecile Andrews has written *The Circle of Simplicity: Return to the Good Life,* which can act as a compendium of advice and insight. Michael Crosby, O.F.M.CAP., states that if while preaching he personalizes his own story and his own "sins" related to his lifestyle, "people seem much more open to listen rather than being given a bunch of statistics about the rich getting richer and the poor poorer."[2]

Wonders of Creation

Preachers need to point out the wonders of our creation that are endless: air, water, soil, sunshine, moon, stars, the multiple variety of species. How many of us know that rye plants have roots stretching seven thousand miles, growing three miles in a day? Or that it would take one million earths to fill our sun, or that the black holes are so deep they could swallow up stars? No wonder the psalmist could exclaim:

> The heavens declare the glory of God;
>   the sky proclaims its builder's craft.
> One day to the next conveys that message;
>   one night to the next imparts that knowledge (19:1-3).

The Catechism of the Catholic Church states that the seventh commandment enjoins "justice and charity in the care of earthly goods."[3]

We need to alert our listeners to what is happening to our earth as often as the Scriptures present this opportunity. The extreme is to preach relentlessly on the topic despite the fact the Scriptures don't lend themselves to this theme. If the Scriptures deal with baptism, we might use the occasion to preach on how precious water is and how much we depend on it. We are able to get along without food for some length of time, but not water. Future wars might be fought over water rights. Even a homily on love of neighbor might include our earth as our neighbor. Remember when Jesus was asked, "Who is my neighbor?" Some preachers tell stories about animals and their love for them as well as for all of creation. Our listeners will often sense our concern and respond accordingly.

One preacher used the following in a sermon:

> Last week I was watching a program on television about gorillas in which it was mentioned that there are only 650 of them still living in the wild. 650 gorillas left! Such a small number. They could fit in this room [it was a cathedral]. It is enough to make one weep.[4]

Needless to say most of the remarks afterwards were about the gorillas. But it forcefully drove home a point.

What Is Happening to the Earth?

Preachers need to talk about their own feelings concerning what is happening to the earth. Bishop Robert Morneau stated his feelings when he compared our planet to a killing field. In the midst of our unprecedented wealth and economic prosperity, Harvard economist Juliet Schor maintains we are less happy than twenty years ago, and more prone to depression. Many eco-psychologists point out the close relationship of our own health and the planet's health. We cannot restore one without the other. Matthew Fox has written:

> When we tear down forests, despoil the soil and the fisheries, the
> ozone layer, and other species—we are destroying ourselves. We
> are living in the greatest period of destruction of the last 60 mil-
> lion years and the truth must be told: anthropocentric religion
> contributes to this devastation. Where creation is, Christ is. And
> where creation is killed, Christ is being crucified all over again.[5]

The Church has to teach that the Earth is our first revelatory experience and that we need to create an intimacy with it. A recent
United Nations study stated that diseases related to polluted environment and unsanitary living conditions kill 35,000 children
daily. This is especially true of third world countries with children
under the age of five.

The feast of St. Francis of Assisi is an excellent time to assert
the value of the earth. Francis, who is the patron of ecology, had a
tremendous love of all creation, not just the birds (too often he is
pictured with a bird bath!). Many stories have been told about his
relation to animals, especially the taming of the wolf of Gubbio.
His "Canticle to the Sun" could act as a powerful way to dramatize
this point or as a fitting conclusion to the homily.

The ark experience for Noah and his family, according to
Rabbinic tradition, gave him an opportunity for a laboratory experience. He spent an entire year taking care of the animals. Some
rabbis believe he was so busy that he did not have much time to
sleep! Imagine the attention and nurturing demanded of him and
all the patience involved in caring for these creatures. No wonder
Noah is described as a man who "walked with God" (Gen 6:10).
Contrast this with what the prophet Hosea spoke of as a result of
greed and injustice, "The beasts of the field, the birds of the air,
and even the fish of the sea perish" (4:3).

Creation Stories

Creation stories in the Bible lend themselves to preaching on
the environment. The Easter vigil might be an opportune time at
least to mention the subject. What might strike us is how God entrusted to us what God has made: "Have dominion over the fish of

the sea, the birds of the air, and all the living things that move on the earth" (Gen 1:28). But this dominion means we need to recognize the fragility of creation and our need to act as responsible stewards. We do not stand as masters of the earth but we are tied to the earth in an intricate network. Preachers make listeners aware that we just don't live on the earth, but we are its caretakers. The earth is our workbench. Abraham Heschel warned that by forfeiting our sense of awe we make the universe a marketplace for ourselves.

We need to present some of the thorny questions like: Does having dominion over the earth enable us to expand our usable space, whether it is used for work or play, especially when it endangers other earth's species? Does the extinction of other species create an imbalance in nature that might eventually lead to our extinction? Gardner Taylor in his *Lyman Beecher Lectures* said, "God gave us dominion over fish and fowl, but not over each other."[6] So the challenge we preachers need to present is how we are to live on God's earth with regard to race, gender, language, or religious persuasion. Indeed, a sobering challenge.

Only when we delight in earth's goodness will we take proper care of it. Norman Wirzba expressed it well:

> Creation is something we are to become, a process that requires of us that we walk with our creator in delighting in and taking care of the good things that are made. In this work we promote relations of joy and peace with the rest of creation and with our God. Moreover, in our nurture of the earth we reflect and embody God's presence on earth.[7]

We read in Genesis "The LORD God then took the man and settled him in the garden of Eden, to cultivate and care for it" (2:15). Taking care of the earth is not an incidental part of our lives. We need to emphasize to our listeners how our existence goes hand in hand with nurturing our earth. So we need to learn more about our environment, but not like we learn the multiplication tables. The answer is not establishing a course in our schools, but that ecology is seen more clearly in relationship to other courses. We admit to suicide, homicide, and genocide, but do we admit to biocide, a killing of our earth? Are we concerned as much about earth economy as we are about human economy? Have we become autistic in our rapport with the earth? Paton's words that if we destroy our land, we destroy ourselves may haunt us. Paula D'Arcy's *Gift of the Red Bird* warns that what is more bothersome is how we destroy our land in such a casual, non-chalant way. We end up abusing what we should respect, and do so with a clear conscience.

Imaginative Approach

Each week (maybe more often if we preach at daily Mass) we face the challenge of creating a homily that speaks to the minds and hearts of our listeners. Maybe what might help us get excited about such a project is to look upon this task as an act of creation or imagination. We sometimes start our homily with a *tohu v'vohu*. Imagination or creativity ought to be a welcome guest in our household. Many preachers feel uncomfortable when challenged to be imaginative. Does the problem arise because theology deals with truth, and imagination deals with dreams, fantasies, and illusions? Henry Ward Beecher considered imagination the most important prerequisite for forceful preaching. He named it a kind of God-power in one's soul, the ability to conceive things which are invisible to our senses. In *Starting from Scratch,* Rita Mae Brown writes, "The process of writing, any form of creativity, is a power intensifying life."[8]

Since preaching on the environment is often challenging, an imaginative approach might accomplish far more than stating a litany of facts. We could enumerate how many rain forests are being cut down at the rate of one football field every second. Eighteen billion tons of topsoil are lost every year; we are running out of usable farm land, no thanks to our money-making methods of agriculture and the boom in housing. Cars and factories are ruining the atmosphere; pesticides are ruining our sources of water. Eighty-two billion tons of toxic waste are injected into the earth's bloodstream. An estimated 65 to 80 percent of our illnesses are attributed to our environment.

Imaginative preaching, however, often paints vivid pictures that remain with the listeners for a long time. So when we feel the resistance to be creative or imaginative we need to balance that with the impact that such a homily might have. Thomas Berry, an outstanding ecotheologian, creatively helped his congregation by saying, "Imagine living on the moon and looking at the essentially flat and formless lunar landscape. If our planet's landscape were as barren as the moon's, our image of the divine would be just as barren. We derive our image of the divine from the natural order."

"The environmental crisis is fundamentally a spiritual crisis," he insists. "And sadly, the churches are for the most part silent. They seem to fail to grasp its spiritual dimension." Berry uses biblical imagery about humanity being at the crossroads, "We are now at a critical moment in evolutionary history. Either the human community will leave the desert to enter a new age, either it will live in harmony with the natural order, or both will perish in the desert." He tells his audiences to listen carefully to these words, "The universe is a communion of subjects, not a collection of objects."[9] He believes that these phrases unlock the secrets of relationship, proportion, humility, awe, and prayer. Berry preaches that we need to become really aware of the sacredness of all relationships, and that would result in us living in harmony and love. He maintains that our main task is to save the planet from destruction.

Our Relationship to Nature

Once we understand our relationship with nature we will cut back on the modern appliances often used. An example might be food processors. Surely it does take more time to chop up things by hand. Many people fall in love with nature by joining an environmental organization. Nature teaches us many lessons about cooperation: bees fertilize flowers, droppings from rabbits create better soil for plants. Nature bonds but does not cling. Did you ever notice how trees bond with plant life? Nature hikes, bird watching, cleaning up parks are wholesome for us. The more concern we have for nature the more this becomes second nature. According to Thomas Wolfe, some of our outstanding miracles not only happen in nature, but also with regularity. Jesus' love of nature is evidenced by his references to the birds of the air, the lilies of the field, the sower and the seed, going to deserted places and up a high mountain.

During the Jubilee Year preachers were invited to help their listeners become more environmentally sensitive. Jubilee is a clarion call to allow the land to lie fallow. Every seventh day the people as well as the domestic animals had to refrain from work to celebrate the Sabbath.

Besides some of the ways already mentioned, we might encourage our listeners to share a newspaper with a neighbor, car pool, cut things in half and consume only half of what we ordinarily eat, save water, use a hand mower instead of an electric one, not buy over-packed goods but buy in bulk, not drive great distances to save a few pennies (remember the saying, is this trip really necessary?), avoid as much as possible disposable articles like diapers. Gardening puts us in contact with the earth and is also very healthy.

Help from Others

Some preachers find it most helpful to discuss their homily with a group of lay people, which can be a rich source of input. The more diverse the group the better. One preacher was helped by a woman who loved gardening. She described God as the gardener who carefully creates the natural world comparable to the way she plants a garden. A man expressed his sorrow about what we are doing to the earth. "We hurt other humans and waste the environment, treating creatures as if all were disposable." A young mother commenting on "have dominion" pointed to the child in her lap and said, "God's dominion is like a loving parent taking care of what is tender and innocent, like my infant daughter. That is the way we should have dominion over the created world. Instead, we interpret dominion to mean use it and abuse it." These insights and similar ones can prove very helpful in creating our homily. Often statements like these will reinforce our own ideas of how God directs and guides the earth.

Our task is not to induce a paralysis of despair when we preach on this topic, especially by moralizing on it. Mere knowledge of the problem can create paralysis. We need to energize our listeners to tackle the problem, which might demand the patience of a Noah and his nurturing care for the animals. We challenge our listeners to live in God's world and to praise and thank God for the wonders God has created. We play a prophetic role in helping others to nurture the earth. Care for the earth is really a form of reverencing God. By doing this we are not only carrying out our civic duty but also an act of worship which unites us most intimately with our Creator.

Notes

[1] Pastoral Statement of the Catholic Bishops of Florida, "Companions in Creation" (January 1, 1991).

[2] Michael Crosby, "Living Compassionately in a Consumer Culture," *New Theology Review* (May 2000) 24.

[3] Catechism of the Catholic Church (Liguori, Mo.: Liguori Publications, 1994) no. 2401.

[4] Nancy Bloomer, "Preaching to Heal the Earth and to Heal Each Other," *Living Pulpit* (April–June 2000) 41.

[5] Matthew Fox, "Celebrating Creation as Blessing," *Living Pulpit* (April–June 2000) 18.

[6] Marvin A. McMickle, "Preaching on the Themes in the Creation Story" *Living Pulpit* (April–June 2000) 43.

[7] Norman Wirzba, "Noah and the Ark: Becoming Creation," *Living Pulpit* (April–June 2000) 29.

[8] "Quotations on the Many Views of Creation," *Living Pulpit* (April–June 2000) 32.

[9] Thomas Berry, "Imagining Living on the Moon," *National Catholic Reporter* (September 6, 1991) 21.

Chapter 7

Do We Heal When We Preach?

We read in the Acts of the Apostles how the early Christians who were persecuted would pray, "And now, Lord, take note of their threats, and enable your servants to speak your word with all boldness, as you stretch forth [your] hand to heal, and signs and wonders are done through the name of your holy servant Jesus" (4:29-30). It becomes evident that they did not pray in order to preach and heal, but to preach through healing. The early Christians preached a powerful message by continuing the works of Jesus. Wasn't this one of the purposes of Luke's writing the Acts, to show how Jesus' message was lived out in the early Church? Is this one reason why much of our preaching today is so abstract and often irrelevant? We can easily preach the doctrine of salvation without the salvation happening. Or a doctrine of healing without believing that healing that can happen. Do we risk healing when we preach?

In reading the Acts of the Apostles we notice how Peter and Paul preached by healing individuals. In fact, there are similarities in their healings: both of them healed a lame man (3:8; 14:8); Peter healed a paralytic (9:34) and Paul the man in bed (28:8); Peter's shadow heals the sick (5:15), handkerchiefs and aprons touched by Paul heal (19:12); Peter revives Dorcas (9:40), Paul raises Eutychus who had fallen out of the window (20:10). We are told in this story how Paul "talked on and on." Eutychus was overcome by sleep. This is another incentive for preachers not to talk or preach on and on, especially when we are repeating ourselves.

Francis MacNutt believes "that the attitude of most Christians today in regard to healing is more shaped by pagan thought than by Christianity—that most sermons on sickness and suffering reflect more the influence of Roman stoicism than the doctrine of the church's Founder."[1]

Jesus the Healer

One-fifth or 20 percent of the Gospels deal with the healing ministry of Jesus. Jesus treated spiritual and physical ills as an enemy. We often talk about "saving souls." Where in the New Testament does it speak about Jesus "saving souls"? Jesus came to heal both body and soul.

What becomes very obvious in the Gospels is that Jesus healed more people than he forgave. Surely he had the power to do both as was true with the paralytic when Jesus said, "Which is easier, to say, 'Your sins are forgiven,' or to say, 'Rise and walk'?" (Matt 9:5). James encourages us, "Confess your sins to one another and pray for one another, that you may be healed" (5:16).

Over the centuries there was a gradual decline in Christ's healing ministry due mainly to Platonic, Stoic, and Manichaen influences. They viewed the body as a prison confining the spirit and hindering spiritual growth. The Desert Fathers viewed the body as something to be tamed and mortified. Some of these influences persist even today. Like everything else there is a grain of truth in all of this, but we need to emphasize in our preaching the holistic approach to the spiritual life. Our bodies are not our enemies.

Some of us might have come in contact with a person suffering from a disease who felt guilty in asking for healing. This individual is often convinced that God wants him or her to suffer and offer up the suffering. Some of this thinking might result from reading the lives of the saints or even from making a retreat or hearing a homily.

I remember reading how Anthony de Mello believed that we need to see every injustice inflicted on us as planned as well as even controlled by God. He maintained that we should go further than "God permitted it," but believe that God plans and controls all that happens to us. This type of reasoning, although well intentioned, is often very confusing and upsetting to many people. It is comparable to telling people when they suffer that it is God's will. Are we in a position to know God's will? Father Peter McCall, O.F.M.CAP., who has given a number of healing retreats at our retreat center in Appleton, maintains that one of the biggest obstacles to healing consists in accepting suffering as God's will. He preaches that this kind of resignation snuffs out the gift of healing.

Redemptive suffering, however, is using suffering to serve some other purpose. Much does depend on our attitude. What a difference when our attitude is that everything happening to us can be meaningful, have a purpose, be significant, convey a message, and be instructional or provide an opportunity for further learning. The basic question we need to ask ourselves is, "What did I learn from the experience?"

No Separation Between Body and Soul

Preachers need to emphasize how we are not separated into body and soul, and that our bodies are not imprisoned in our souls. God is concerned not just with our souls but our bodies as well. Jesus demonstrated that salvation is meant for the whole person. In Matthew's Gospel, after Jesus cured a leper, a centurion's servant, and Peter's mother-in-law, we read, "When it was evening, they brought him many who were possessed by demons, and he drove out the spirits by a word and cured all the sick, to fulfill what had been said by Isaiah the prophet: 'He took away our infirmities and bore our diseases'" (Matt 8:16-17).

Healing is like preaching if we understand it as ministering love to suffering and burdened people. As Jesus ministered to both spirit and body, we also minister to both spirit and body by our healing and preaching. It is not an either/or; but truly a both/and.

Jesus became like us in all things except sin, as St. Paul said, so we might become like him especially as we preach and heal as he did. Our task is to put on Christ and reflect him by our preaching as Paul did.

If doctors, nurses, and others minister to make people well, trying to carry out Christ's command to help the sick, why is that at times some preachers persuade their listeners to carry their cross and not ask for healing? Jesus sent out his twelve apostles "and gave them authority over unclean spirits to drive them out and to cure every disease and every illness" (Matt 10:1). Jesus also said:

> These signs will accompany those who believe: in my name they will drive out demons, they will speak new languages. They will pick up serpents [with their hands], and if they drink any deadly thing, it will not harm them. They will lay hands on the sick, and they will recover (Mark 16:17-18).

This same command has been given to us. Only then will we be able to understand how the healing ministry of Jesus was not just "signs and wonders." They forcefully bring out the Gospel message or Good News which we are to proclaim by our preaching. Jesus is truly the loving, compassionate healer who dispelled demons and restored people to health. He challenges us to allow that reign of God Jesus proclaimed to come more alive in the world and thereby destroy the reign of evil.

The Church often relegates the healing ministry to what are considered more competent professionals. Preachers definitely should be considered competent in this field. Many clergy and some lay people limit their role to visitation, a brief prayer, and support of the sick. Have we lost Jesus' vitality in the healing ministry? If we believe that body and soul are connected as well as health and religion, we would be like Jesus and know healing is close at hand?

In Jesus' time people frequented synagogues because they believed some change from God could take place. The scribes and Pharisees were the biggest obstacles to change. Jesus healed in their synagogues. One of the outstanding examples is the man with an unclean spirit (Mark 1:23-27). Is it not ironic that such a person be present in a synagogue on a Sabbath? Up until Jesus enters the synagogue the man was comfortable. He, not the scribes and Pharisees, is the person who recognizes Jesus: "I know who you are—the Holy One of God!" Jesus brought a holiness which drives out the unclean spirit. Now the synagogue has become a place which differentiates Jesus and the Pharisees. He healed and they could not. What do we bring to the liturgy and the preaching event?

Faith Needed

Most experts in the healing ministry point out the necessity of faith. The reason becomes evident when we see Jesus in action in the Gospels and how often he rewards the faith of the person healed like Bartimaeus: "Go your way; your faith has saved you" (Mark 10:52). And to the woman suffering from a hemorrhage for twelve years: "Courage, daughter! Your faith has saved you" (Matt 9:22). But what about people who respond "yes" when they are asked, "Do you have faith to be healed?" Often the sick are not cured and are told that it was because of their weak faith.

Patrick McDonald, a licensed clinical social worker, told the story of a charismatic priest at a conference he attended. The priest was flawlessly dressed in a white robe and passionately told his listeners that Jesus would heal any and every one of their diseases as long as the person had deep faith. McDonald pointed out that, despite the priest's theatrical presentation, his theology of healing was much too simplistic and flawed.

Needless to say McDonald left the conference very angry. One of his close friends was upset because he was not healed and was convinced it was due to his lack of faith. McDonald felt it was a perfect example of manipulation, especially since the healings were attributed to the healer's gifts. Such an approach also adds skepticism to those who do not believe in the healing ministry. Being involved in the healing ministry can be an experience of power. The same is true of preaching. Since power can corrupt or be addictive, healing can lead to manipulation and control.

Paul Tournier believes that the popular preacher or evangelist has a tendency to simplify healing by saying, "If you have faith, you will be healed."[2] We need to be open to however God wants to heal, not the way we anticipate it to happen. God works in mysterious and unexpected ways. There is a story of a religious sister who asked for healing of her knees because she was confined to a wheel chair. While a team prayed over her, she suddenly put her hands to her face. She was healed of her facial paralysis which she had not asked about. Later her knees were healed, enabling her to walk. Indeed, the healing process is mysterious.

Kathryn Kuhlman, a famous minister of healing, has seen many people hurt and made to feel guilty because they were not healed. She concluded that she did not know why some people were healed and others were not. What amazed her is how people with deep faith came to her services and were not healed, and some skeptics were. Truly it is another one of God's mysteries to be lived and not solved.

Barbara Shlemon, who has been involved in the healing ministry, maintains that there are numerous reasons why people are not healed. She insists also that only God knows the reasons. After many years in the ministry of healing she has stopped asking why all people aren't healed. Barbara now directs her attention to those who need healing, leaving the results in God's hands who, as she says, is still very much in control of the universe.

Healing and Curing

A distinction might also be made between a cure and healing. Joel Giallanza, c.s.c., writes that "healing has to do with quality of life, touching every dimension of personal life. Curing has to do with removing identified disruptions in the soundness of physical or mental or emotional life functions."[3] Jesus cured many people who were deaf, blind, mute, and possessed by demons. We don't know how many were healed by means of an ongoing process much like the man who gradually regained his sight and said, "I see people looking like trees and walking" (Mark 8:24). Jesus cured the man who came from the tombs and had an unclean spirit (Mark 5:1-20). Once the man was cured he pleaded with Jesus to be allowed to go with Jesus. Jesus did not allow him to follow or join his company, but told him, "Go home to your family and announce to them all that the Lord in his pity has done for you." This definitely was not a healing but a cure, but why didn't Jesus automatically allow the man to be his disciple?

The healing might also take another form. People who pilgrimage to Lourdes are often cured. The many crutches left and recorded miracles are convincing proof. However, many are healed rather than cured. Maybe the greater miracle or a deepening of their faith happens when people accept their illness and allow God to heal them in another way.

We need to challenge our listeners to move forward in a creative, healing way, otherwise they will resist the opportunity for healing as the scribes and Pharisees did. All of us need to see ourselves as God intended, people open to the healing power of Jesus. Openness to God and deepening that relationship will ensure our own healing as well as others. Individuals who wear masks or look very pious and religious like the Scribes and Pharisees short circuit the healing process.

The Blind

The people most frequently healed by Jesus were the blind. Jesus made it very clear that illness is not always connected with sin in the story of the man who was blind from birth (John 9). Jesus gave the answer we need to preach, "so that the works of God might be made visible through him" (v. 3). God's purposes are not always clear and are often mysterious. Jesus goes on to say to his apostles and us, "We have to do the works of the one who sent me while it is day. Night is coming when no one can work" (v. 4). We are given the day to work and the night to rest. (Unless of course one is on a night shift!) For Jesus the night was the cross which lay ahead. We are given only so much valuable time to preach a healing message as Jesus did. If we misuse this opportunity we can be like the Scribes and Pharisees who claimed to see and yet did not see. That is the greater sin.

Sickness

We need to preach how sickness can be an opportunity for grace depending on how we respond to the illness. There are many people like A. J. Cronin, who wanted to be a medical doctor but because of his illness was unable to pursue this profession. He took up writing and became famous. Many have turned their lives around because of sickness or some tragic accident. For many pain or sickness has a tendency to turn them in on themselves or to indulge in self-pity, so there is a greater need for them not to look upon themselves as victims of an illness or disease. We are given a choice of becoming a better person or a bitter person as a result of the sickness or tragedy.

In *The Healing Power of Illness,* Thorwald Dethlefsen and Rudiger Dahlke show how most people who are ill are not innocent victims of nature, but are authors of their own sicknesses. Symptoms of their sicknesses are shown as "bodily expressions of psychological conflicts."[4] For example, asthmatics have a tendency to take too much or are domineering; liver sufferers often lose their sexual potency; aggression is a symptom of gallstones; anorexics exaggerate the ascetic ideal; kidney problems arise when people are in conflict with others.

Wayne Dyer has written a book entitled *There's a Spiritual Solution to Every Problem* in which he shows the need to tap into our own healing energy. He suffered a heart attack and wrote:

> Now it is up to me. I am not this body; I am a spiritual being, eternal, always connected to God. I could shift my awareness to being the observer rather than the victim, which is what I have been writing about over the past twenty years. It was as if the light came on in a dark room. I felt the presence of a higher, faster healing energy almost immediately. I began to be cheerful rather than morose. I circulated

around the cardiac ward attempting to cheer up those who were much worse off than myself. I began to view the hospital and many healing professionals with awe, love and respect rather than with thoughts of fear and anxiety. I looked for what was right about that place and experienced gratitude for everything my senses witnessed. . . . Surely the presence of God is in this place.[5]

We can thank God that today more and more people are not surrendering to their sickness, but are seeking other alternatives, especially healing and prayer. The advice given by St. Ignatius still makes good sense in the area of healing: We need to pray like everything depended on God, but work like all depended on us.

Jesus gave his disciples "authority over unclean spirits to drive them out and to cure every disease and every illness" (Matt 10:1). Do we believe we have that authority and God wants people to be healed? If all healing is spiritual healing and we are spirited preachers, we should be able to carry on the work of Jesus' healing ministry. For, "Jesus Christ is the same yesterday, today, and forever" (Heb 13:8).

Notes

[1] Francis MacNutt, *Healing* (Huntington, Ind.: Ave Maria Press, 1999) 49.

[2] Ibid., 108.

[3] Joel Giallanza, "Spirituality for Religious in Health Care Ministry," *Human Development* (Spring 1994) 26–7.

[4] Thorwald Dethlefsen and Rudiger Dahlke, *The Healing Power of Illness*, trans. Peter Lemesurer (Rockport, Mass.: Element, Inc., 1990) vii.

[5] Wayne W. Dyer, *There's a Spiritual Solution to Every Problem* (New York: Harper Collins, 2001) xii.

Chapter 8

How to Preach on Ageing

Isn't it startling that we don't find any Gospel texts dealing with the call to grow old? We do find a passage in Ephesians on how to grow up: "so that we may no longer be infants, tossed by waves and swept along by every wind of teaching. . . . Rather, living the truth in love, we should grow in every way into him who is the head, Christ . . ." (4:14-15). St. Paul exhorted the Corinthians not be discouraged: "although our outer self is wasting away, our inner self is being renewed day by day" (2 Cor 4:16). That is what we need to preach on ageing because it is in direct contrast to our culture today. Indeed, that is risky and challenging.

If ageing involves the total experience from birth to death, preachers need to know the various aspects of ageing in order to preach on them. King David's youth and ageing process is a fascinating story. One preacher gave a well-received series of sermons on Jesus' childhood, adolescence, and adulthood using Luke 2. Some might object saying, "What do we know about Jesus' teen years beyond twelve and leading up to his public life?" This can challenge a preacher's imagination and creativity. One way is to watch for fascinating stories of elderly people. Recall the lady in Paris a few years ago who died at age 122. She rode a bicycle at 100 and produced a CD at 121. Erik Erikson published two books at the age of 87. Since preachers face listeners with a wide age span or multicultural background, another way to be creative is to encourage them to put themselves in someone else's shoes. It might be possible for youths to identify with middle aged, or the middle aged could envision themselves in the elders' positions. And if done well, compassion and empathy might result.

A focus on "The Third Age" is far more meaningful to the ageing than speaking of them as people who are retired. This term avoids the fixed criteria often applied to the elderly. A Third Age Center was established at Fordham University in New York City back in 1978. People are evaluated according to personal capacity rather than chronological age. The Third Age enables individuals to establish new opportunities, roles, relationships, and skills which can be a special force for good in our society. Most elderly want to be useful and get around physically.

Isolation

Isolation is definitely one of the areas that can plague the elderly. We will not find isolation listed as a disease in medical journals, but there is proof isolation contributes to illness. Serious isolation usually results in major problems. We can remind our listeners what God said in the creation story: "It is not good for the man to be alone. I will make a suitable partner for him" (Gen 2:18). This passage implies that it is not good for people to isolate themselves. They need to stitch themselves into the lives of others. Caroline Heilbrun wrote about life beyond the sixties and what she had acquired "after a lifetime of solitude and few close and constant companions, women friends and colleagues, themselves now mature adults, whose intimacy helped to make the 60s my happiest decade."[1]

We live in a society where ageing is denied and the young often will not have anything to do with elders. In some instances ageing people are not invited into discussions or plans of those younger than themselves. Maybe a worse tragedy occurs when the elderly shun their own. It happened where an elderly woman looking into a gathering of senior members said, "I don't want to go in there. There are too many old people." Such gatherings play an important role in the lives of these precious people.

Many elderly, however, desire better awareness of their needs—the need to be accepted and for better communication. They do not want to be relegated into the background or considered a piece of furniture in a room. They wish their children would be able to take care of them and not consign them so easily into a nursing home. I remember visiting a home-bound lady whose son built a section onto his house where his mother could live, feel part of the family, and yet enjoy some independence. One of the saddest things I hear when visiting nursing homes is that family and friends rarely come to visit many of the residents. Even a phone call can be so meaningful to them. Preachers need to encourage listeners to be aware of this problem.

A powerful way to implement this awareness is by setting a good example within the parish. Many parishes have someone in charge of visiting the homebound or people in nursing homes or hospices. Couples married fifty to sixty years or more renewing their wedding vows can be a touching event for the young and middle aged. Some parishes sponsor educational events, social activities, Bible studies, and justice projects. One parish initiated a program called "ageless friends." The volunteers were paired with people twenty years younger than themselves. They met once a month wherever they decided to converse with each other. Some theological students had the assignment of talking and listening to elderly people in a nursing home. One of the students asked, "What if they can't talk or hear or are unconscious?" The response was, "You still do the same."

Angela Sturgill tells the story of how she volunteered as a candy striper for thirty to forty hours a week at a local hospital. Most of the time she spent holding the hand of Mr. Gillespie, who was in a coma. Nobody visited him or seemed to care about his condition. She had to leave for a week's vacation and when she returned, he was gone. She feared he was dead and did not want to inquire further. Several years later she saw a man at a gas station who looked like Mr. Gillespie. It was! After she told him who she was, he gave her the warmest hug she ever received. He then told her how her voice and touch kept him alive.

In *Toward Holy Ground* Margaret Guenther maintains, "Each of those very old people, no matter how fragile their hold on life might be and no matter how useless they might be in the eyes of society, is a rare parchment. A rare parchment waiting to be read."[2] Preachers need to interpret that parchment with fresh insights. As the psalmist declares concerning the palm tree, "They shall bear fruit even in old age, / always vigorous and sturdy" (92:15).

Traditions

It is enlightening to examine the various traditions that different races have toward ageing. India refers to the first half of one's life as the "household stage." Once that is passed the second half is devoted to one's spiritual development. African Americans hold their elders in high esteem. Older women are still addressed as mother and maintain much influence. The veneration for older men who are called dads and wise men is very evident. For southern Ghana's Akans, ageing is wisdom which demands reverence and respect. Honoring the aged for the Native Americans brings life and wisdom. Confucians connect their respect for elders as an intricate moral principal in their lives which brings peace and order to the world. Confucius taught that in youth one must guard against lust; in middle age, aggressive acts to reach one's goal; and in old age, avarice, hanging on to our possessions and life itself.

Hindu tradition does not emphasize the physical weakness of the elderly but their spiritual maturity. Buddhists regard ageing as moving toward a fuller life. The Jewish tradition stresses that the elderly are fundamental to life. They contribute more to society than the young. Rabbi Shlomo Balter states, "Important affairs are not necessarily performed by muscle, speed and nimbleness, but by reflection, character and judgment—all of which are considered difficult in a world filled with the racket of push and pull, where speed and youth are equipped with good."[3] The Japanese accentuate the seasons of the year and associate them with the seasons of life, each bringing its own beauty. Inner tranquility is a sign for them of one's later years. All of these and similar traditions have left their footprints embedded in the sands of time. Many experts maintain that the culture and especially the prosperity of a country will be determined by how the aged are treated.

Challenge of Ageing

We need to make our listeners aware how ageing can be a time of growth, especially spiritually, experiencing and celebrating God's presence anew. The struggles, pains, and aches of the elderly might be their way to find God more present in their lives. The enemy will use all kinds of disguises like frustration, anger, loneliness, and despair to confuse them.

Abraham Joshua Heschel expressed it well:

> Being old is not necessarily the same as being stale. The effort to restore the dignity of old age will depend upon our ability to revive the equation of old age and wisdom. Wisdom is the substance upon which the inner security of the old will forever depend. But the attainment of wisdom is the work of a lifetime. Just to be is a blessing. Just to live is holy.[4]

It is easy for preachers to tell this to others, but we need to apply it to ourselves, as Henri Nouwen states:

> Our first question is not how to go out and help the elderly, but how to allow the elderly to enter into the center of our own lives, how to create the space where they can be heard and listened to from within with careful attention. Quite often our concern to preach, teach or cure prevents us from perceiving and receiving what those we care for have to offer.[5]

Fr. Walter Burghardt, s.j., is eighty-seven years young and identifies with the psalmist:

> Seventy is the sum of our years,
>   or eighty, if we are strong. . . .
> They pass quickly, we are but gone (90:10).

He comments, "Bones become brittle, joints jab, oxygen reaches the heart more slowly, and sauerkraut makes for diarrhea. Writing, lecturing, preaching—the days slip by all too swiftly. All the more reason to be a living witness to God's presence—a witness seasoned by wisdom, enhanced by grace."[6]

C. G. Jung states that the second half of our lives is meant to turn inward toward spiritual development or what he calls "individuation," reaching one's full potential. Ageing people become more aware that they are pilgrims and wayfarers on a march, and are called to a kenosis or self-emptying, letting go of many of their prized possessions. Recently I saw one of our friars hand over the keys to his car to the local minister because he discerned that he should not drive in the future. Jesus said to Peter, "Amen, amen, I say to you, when you were younger, you used to dress yourself and go where you wanted; but when you grow old, you will stretch out your hands, and someone else will dress you and lead you where you do not want to go" (John 21:18).

The elderly certainly are challenged to matriculate in the school of hard knocks. This school teaches them how to become more like Christ, which is an endless process, one that will not fully be completed here on earth. From the womb to the tomb there is a constant clarion call for them to let go, which increases steadily with age. Elders can mellow, become more loving and compassionate, or grow more cynical, crabby, irritable, and pessimistic. They become their choices. They relive the paschal mystery of Jesus in a concrete way and are intimately united to his sufferings, especially on the cross. As someone has said, "We have to look good on wood." In this daring adventure they become more and more like Christ and are able to say with Paul, "I have been crucified with Christ; yet I live, no longer I, but Christ lives in me" (Gal 2:19-20).

In *The Force of Character and the Lasting Life* James Hillman has a similar approach that the second half of their lives the elderly should center on developing their "character" or the wholesome qualities they possess. These will become more manifested in their faces and, tongue in cheek, he believes that plastic surgery ought to be outlawed. Hellman insists that wisdom is found in the problems, and that the aches and pains provide symbolic messages. For example, a stiff neck might indicate that a person is too rigid or dogmatic.

Most people will agree that our society places top priority on youth even though the book of Proverbs states, "The glory of young men is their strength, / and the dignity of old men is gray hair" (20:29). Some elderly find it difficult to accept their finiteness or accept the reality of ageing and death. William Stringfellow referred to the fear of ageing as the "idolatry of death," considering it a predominant problem in our culture. Funeral homilies and wakes can offer an excellent opportunity to stress these human conditions. Instead of accepting the ageing process, which cannot be halted, many opt for plastic surgery in an attempt to stay young. Betty Friedan in *The Fountain of Age* maintains that we deny ageing and death more than we deny resistance to feminism.

Ageing: A Paradox

The ageing process is indeed a paradox. Dorothy Sayers states, "Paradoxical as it may seem, to believe in youth is to look backward; to look forward we must believe in age."[7] They are given a choice to move steadily toward a deeper union with God, or find life meaningless, boring, and frustrating. How often we hear of a person who seems to have everything—money, power, fame—but ends his or her life in despair. The opposite can also be true: someone with very little who knows even less lives a fulfilling life. As the psalmist says:

> God, you have taught me from my youth;
> > to this day I proclaim your wondrous deeds.
> Now that I am old and gray,
> > do not forsake me, God (71:17-18).

Our own mortality and finiteness are held in juxtaposition. Elderly who have a pessimistic attitude toward life need to read Pope John Paul II's homily "Jubilee of the Elderly," where he states, "The Church looks with love and trust upon you elderly people,

dedicating herself to encouraging the fulfillment of a human, social and spiritual context in which every person can live this important stage of his life fully and with dignity."[8] The apostle Paul
affirms that God, who gives life to the dead (Rom 4:17), will also
give life to our mortal bodies (8:11). Jimmy Carter, in his book on
ageing, writes that one of the signs of maturity is to accept hon-
estly our frustrated dreams, disability, illnesses, and eventual
death as the normal facets of one's life. Despite these ordeals the
elderly can continue to grow, learn, and be challenged by them.
Emily Dickinson wrote, "We turn not older with years, but newer
every day."[9]

Cyclical

Too often we see or interpret ageing in a linear rather than a
cyclical way. Teilhade Chardin believed that all life was an ascend-
ing spiral, individuals as well as communities moving toward a
"Christification" or a union with God. Grace moves us upward
and anxiety pulls us downward. Paul tells us of his cyclical journey
in all the sufferings he experienced (2 Cor 11:23-29) and how he
desired to be relieved of his "thorn in the flesh." His burden did
not change, but to finally accept his weakness (and even boast
about it) was a tremendous grace.

Jesus pointed out the spirals in life when he spoke of the seed
falling into the ground, and at the Last Supper when he told his
disciples, "From now on I shall not drink this fruit of the vine
until the day when I drink it with you new in the kingdom of my
Father" (Matt 26:29). The seed as well as wine take a different and
more perfect form.

Sense of Humor

It is important to stress to the elderly the need to develop or
continue developing a good sense of humor. Nothing can take the
sting out of the harsh realities of ageing than possessing such a
quality. A spry eighty-two-year-old man was asked how he felt at
his age. His response with a smile was, "Well, considering the al-

ternative , I feel pretty good." "I'll never make the mistake of turning 70 again," Casey Stengel said. I remember the elderly man who said to me, "Father, don't get old." My response was, "How do you accomplish that?"

Someone has joked of the elderly that they can have dinner at 4 P.M., kidnappers will not bother them, they can keep your secrets because they can't remember them, things they buy usually do not wear out, they have nothing left to learn the hard way, their arthritis is a far better weather predictor than a meteorologist, they will probably be the first released in a hostage situation, and their favorite songs might be "The Old Rugged Face," "Nobody Knows the Trouble I Have Seen," or "Just a Slower Walk With Thee."

By the year 2030 it is estimated that there will be 66 million people over age sixty-five; they will be the fastest growing demographic in our country. So we better listen to them addressing their problems, because they are the wisdom figures and fountains of tradition. All of us are headed for or are already at the Third Age.

Notes

[1] "Ageing," *Living Pulpit* (January–March 2001) 37.

[2] Margaret Guenther, "A Rare Parchment," *Living Pulpit* (January–March 2001) 9.

[3] Shlomo Balter, "Helping the Ageing Come of Age," *Living Pulpit* (January–March 2001) 13.

[4] Ibid.

[5] Walter J. Burghardt, "To Age Is to Grow," *Living Pulpit* (January–March 2001) 42.

[6] Ibid.

[7] "Quotations on the Many Views of Ageing," *Living Pulpit* (January–March 2001) 33.

[8] Pope John Paul II, "Jubilee of the Elderly," homily given in Rome, September 17, 2000.

[9] "Quotations on the Many Views of Ageing," 33.

Chapter 9

Preaching the Wisdom of Jesus

If we want to understand what the New Testament has to say about Jesus, we need to understand more clearly what wisdom (commonly called *sophia*) is. Luke tells us that Jesus came to Nazareth and "advanced [in] wisdom and age and favor before God and man" (2:52). This bit of information gives us a better understanding of the Incarnation, that Jesus was not omniscient and did not possess the ability to solve all problems. Jesus had to learn from Mary and Joseph just as we have to learn from our parents. He learned from Joseph how to be a carpenter and from Mary how to love. We can only imagine how he grew up, especially as a teenager, and how he related to others. St. Paul referred to Jesus as "Christ the power of God and the wisdom of God" (1 Cor 1:24). Why? Because Jesus, the complete expression of God's wisdom, brought this wisdom among us. Truly he was the teacher of wisdom. Are we willing to risk preaching him as true wisdom?

True wisdom is not knowledge, a library of facts, a plethora of data, or an erudition of a well-versed professor. Wisdom implies the ability to understand, perceive, discern, and use good judgment. It implies a down-to-earth interpretation of life as it is really lived. We often use the term "wisdom figure," referring to someone who can offer sound advice and counsel, someone who has borne the heat of the day. Jesus was truly a "wisdom figure" despite his youth.

True wisdom has a twofold purpose: an invitation to deeper understanding and a wholesome relationship to God, others, and oneself. An important distinction needs to be made to preach wisdom the way Jesus did. Keith Russell maintains, "Wisdom may claim to have truth but it does not claim to be truth."[1] Too many religious groups like fundamentalists claim to possess the truth. Preachers need to respect and love all truth and wisdom which is contained in the person of Jesus.

Marcus J. Borg in *Meeting Jesus Again for the First Time* states, "For early Christianity, Jesus was the son of the Father and the incarnation of Sophia, the child of the intimate Abba, and the child of Sophia."[2] This insight enables the preacher to be more sensitive concerning inclusive language, an important issue for many people today. Elizabeth Johnson writes:

> When at some future date the history of spirituality of this age is written, authors will note the vigor with which women took Sophia into their hearts and lives, allowing her to open new pathways toward divine mystery and finding in her femaleness a validation of their own sacred selves.[3]

Elizabeth Schussler Fiorenza insists that Jesus as the child of Sophia was "sent to gather the children of Israel to their gracious Sophia-God."[4]

Wisdom in Latin is *sapientia*, which is derived from *sapere*, meaning to taste. Spiritual writers like Origen and Bonaventure often wrote about the "spiritual senses" that enable us to know the realities of faith much better. Ignatius' *Spiritual Exercises* exhorts individuals to actually smell God's boundless fragrance and taste God's sweetness. Doesn't the psalmist exclaim, "Learn to savor how good the Lord is" (34:9)?

Preaching God's Wisdom

Our task as preachers is to preach "God's power and God's wisdom" revealed in Jesus (1 Cor 1:24). We need to preach the wisdom that Jesus preached, which is no easy task. We can easily preach the wisdom of the world about which Paul writes (1 Cor 1:21). Are we reluctant to preach on sin, social justice, racism, militarism, and sexism? We read in 2 Timothy, "For the time will come when people will not tolerate sound doctrine, but, following their own desires and insatiable curiosity, will accumulate teachers and will stop listening to the truth and will be diverted to myths" (4:3-4). Has that time come?

Jesus taught a tough kind of wisdom. He opened his mission in the synagogue at Nazareth by stating that he would

> bring glad tidings to the poor. . . .
> Proclaim liberty to captives
> and recovery of sight to the blind,
>   to let the oppressed go free,
> and to proclaim a year acceptable to the Lord (Luke 4:18-19).

This is Jesus' inaugural address just like Peter's sermon on Pentecost (Acts 2:14-41). Jesus was anointed and commissioned to carry out what he proclaimed. And then he had the wisdom to say, "Today this scripture passage is fulfilled in your hearing" (Luke 4:21).

At times we might find it risky or very challenging to preach on thorny issues. We need to recall Jesus' words: "For I myself shall give you a wisdom in speaking that all your adversaries will be powerless to resist or refute" (Luke 21:15). It was this wisdom that enabled Peter and Paul to preach their forceful messages about Jesus.

Jesus: A Deep Thinker

Jesus is portrayed in the Gospels as a deep thinker. He took time to contemplate all things. So we have a multitude of his pensive sayings: proverbs, prophetic words, aphorisms, and parables. The bedrock of his sayings has been passed on in Matthew's Sermon on the Mount or Luke's Sermon on the Plain. His wisdom is advocated in his many "You have heard that it was said to your ancestors, 'You shall not kill; and whoever kills will be liable to judgment.' But I say to you, whoever is angry with his brother [or sister] will be liable to judgment" (Matt 5:21-22). How does this apply to road rage or, now, parent rage? He went on to say, "You have heard that it was said, 'An eye for an eye and a tooth for a tooth.' But I say to you, offer no resistance to one who is evil. When someone strikes you on [your] right cheek, turn the other one to him as well" (Matt 5:38-39). How can anyone strike us on the right cheek without using the back of the hand? That was a worse insult for a Jew. Indeed, these expressions of wisdom are most challenging and will stretch our listeners as well as ourselves.

Wisdom was designated to the scribal class who were well educated. Jesus was a peasant not a scribe, and he was not well educated. That explains why when he preached in the Nazareth synagogue many people were astounded and said in disdain, "Where did this man get all this? What kind of wisdom has been given him? What mighty deeds are wrought by his hands! Is he not the carpenter, the son of Mary . . . ?" (Mark 6:2-3). They took offense at his message and would not listen to him. When Jesus proclaimed to the Jews "I am the bread that came down from heaven," they said, "Is this not Jesus, the son of Joseph? Do we not know his father and mother?" (John 6:41-42).

But Jesus, the carpenter's son, a nobody, was a thinker. His profound thoughts were unsettling. He considered marginal people like tax collectors, prostitutes, lepers, the possessed, and the lame important and not expendable. Jesus wanted his listeners to consider the unclean as clean, and sinners capable of enjoying a meal together. When he saw Zacchaeus perched up in a sycamore tree, he said to him, "Zacchaeus, come down quickly, for today I must stay at your house" (Luke 19:5). Zacchaeus was overjoyed, but the people grumbled and complained that Jesus was going to a sinner's house. This kind of relationship was reserved to friends.

An example of one of his pensive sayings was: "Come to me, all you who labor and are burdened, and I will give you rest. Take my yoke upon you . . ." (Matt 11:28-29). "Yoke" was looked upon as a subordination to God. Rabbis often spoke of the "yoke" of the Torah or the commandments. The "surprise" is not in the juxtaposition of rest and yoke, but rather Jesus' boldness to declare that his yoke will give rest. Is that possible?

Wisdom in the Reign of God and Parables

Jesus discarded much of the conventional wisdom and tried to replace it with a reign of God approach rather than a reign of the Roman Empire. Many of his stories and parables give us a glimpse of what this reign or kingdom of God will be like. "A man gave a great dinner to which he invited many." But there were many no-shows. So he tells his servants to go out into the streets and alleys and bring in the poor, the crippled, and the blind (Luke 14:16-24). Meals were Jesus' favorite means to demonstrate the future of God's kingdom having already arrived. Jesus envisioned the consummation of God's reign in the coming of the Gentiles who will sit at the table with Abraham, Isaac, and Jacob (Matt 8:11). The outsiders become insiders. Those included are now excluded.

Jesus offered a cluster of parables containing much hidden and shocking wisdom. Listeners need to look for another kind of wisdom, one that will enable them to transform their lives and not conform themselves to this age (Rom 12:2). The world makes every effort to have us conform to it. Tremendous pressure is exerted to shape, form, and mold us into its image. Much discipline is needed to counteract these pressures. A good example of someone who did not conform herself was Ms. Eleanor Boyer, a seventy-five-year-old lady who won a 20 million dollar lottery in New Jersey. She gave all the money to her church and charity. She wanted no publicity or even any praise from the pulpit. The monsignor of her parish received more than eight years' of Sunday collections. (How many pastors might sport green eyes and would be elated with a contribution like that!)

As preachers we are challenged to preach in new ways. Jesus' preaching, especially the parables, will stimulate us to look at life more seriously with the lens of wisdom. A landowner hires laborers at different hours of the day and pays them the same amount, bringing out the idea of reversal, "The last will be first, and first will be last" (Matt 20:1-16). This is certainly no way to run a railroad, and we can understand how those hired earlier were angry and upset. But there are other possibilities to consider: "Are you envious because I am generous?" A certain employer out east had the misfortune of his factory burning to the ground. But he decided to continue paying his employees while the factory was rebuilt. What a powerful example of generosity. Maybe those who worked a shorter time accomplished as much as the others. Skillful workers are able to accomplish this.

A man had two sons whom he sent out into his vineyard. One said he would go but did not, and the other refused but later changed his mind and went. Preachers can show how people can make all kinds of promises but not fulfill them. Good talkers abound, but how many are doers? Fine words are never a substitute for fine deeds. Jesus stated that not anyone who says Lord, Lord, will enter the reign of God. People claim to be good, generous, and upright, but actually are not. I remember a married man who berated other Catholics because of the way they lived and acted. Later I found out this man was having an affair with another woman. Jesus said, "Amen, I say to you, tax collectors and prostitutes are entering the kingdom of God before you"(Matt 21:28-31).

The parable of the wheat and the weeds depicts how God's reign is pitted against the reign of evil. As St. Thomas Aquinas points out, evil is nothing; it is the absence of good. And evil is everywhere and comparable to a giant spider web as we have seen. Touch the web anywhere and you set the whole web trembling. Americans comprise about 5 percent of the world's population, but consume 82 percent of the resources. In terms of national gross products we are on top! Yet we give less to charitable organizations. Preachers need to make clear that God is not the cause of evil. We often confuse pain with evil. As the poet Theodora Roethke wrote, in the dark time, the eye begins to see. The tendency, as brought out in the parable, is to root out the weeds. Our task is not to understand the problem of evil and pain but to counteract it wherever possible. There will be a harvest time when the good will be separated from evil. We might even ask our listeners on what side will we be.

We also have the dishonest steward who is commended for acting prudently (Luke 16:1-8). Here a preacher might compare this parable to the prodigal son who squandered his father's property.

The steward's sagacity and brilliance is praised, not his unrighteousness. He was a rascal and could have been a blackmailer. Some years ago New York had a garbage strike. Naturally the garbage mounted. But one man devised a clever way to get rid of his garbage. He wrapped the garbage in exquisitely decorated boxes, and left them in his unlocked car. Needless to say the garbage disappeared without any difficulty. This parable also reminds me of a couple who took their ten-month-old baby along to a movie. They were instructed before going into the theater that if the baby cried, they would have to leave but that their money would be refunded. As the movie progressed, the husband asked the wife what she thought of the movie. "It is horrible," she responded. He said, "Pinch the baby."

Alternative Wisdom

Jesus preached an alternative wisdom which undermined the social boundaries produced by the conventional wisdom of his time. Has that conventional wisdom changed that much today?

Conventional wisdom maintains that God is a punitive lawgiver, whereas alternative wisdom pictures God as gracious and kind. Conventional wisdom pictures a person's worth by what is determined by social standards (how productive are you?), whereas alternative wisdom holds all people have infinite worth as children of God. Conventional wisdom urges people to be first, but the alternative wisdom of Jesus encourages us to be last with the assurance that we will be first.

Conventional wisdom leads to blindness. "If a blind person leads a blind person, both will fall into a pit," Jesus said (Matt 15:14). Jesus' alternative wisdom invites individuals to see differently. The path Jesus offers is radically centered in God, not in culture. Preachers can present any of the conventional wisdom, and then point out how different and challenging alternative wisdom is. What are the implications to center one's life in God rather than in a culture?

Anti-Wisdom

Jesus preached a foolish kind of wisdom often called an anti-wisdom. This kind of wisdom does not fit into the lives of most ordinary listeners, and maybe not into our own lives. The themes that wisdom unravels are seeking and finding. Jesus said, "Whoever wishes to save his life will lose it, but whoever loses his life for my sake and that of the gospel will save it" (Mark 8:35). "Blessed are you when they insult you and persecute you and utter every kind of evil against you [falsely] because of me. Rejoice and be glad, for your reward will be great in heaven" (Matt 5:11-12). "Give to everyone who asks of you, and from the one who takes what is yours do not demand it back" (Luke 6:30). "Love your enemies and do good to them" (Luke 6:35). "It is easier for a camel to pass through [the] eye of [a] needle than for one who is rich to enter the kingdom of God" (Mark 10:25). "If anyone comes to me without hating his father and mother, wife and children, brothers and sisters, and even his own life, he cannot be my disciple" (Luke 14:26). Jesus' subversive wisdom climaxed on the cross. And that is foolishness according to modern standards. But in final analysis it is true wisdom. St. Paul expressed it well, "Let no one deceive himself. If anyone among you considers himself wise in this age, let him become a fool, so as to become wise. For the wisdom of this world is foolishness in the eyes of God" (1 Cor 3:18-19).

We find in these passages the hidden wisdom that will transform our culture and society. But to discover this kind of wisdom demands profound contemplation on the part of a preacher, a deeper understanding of what these words really mean. Mary is often hailed as the "seat of wisdom." She pondered so many words spoken to her in the recesses of her heart. That demanded much contemplation, absorption, and wonderment. She truly is a wisdom figure.

We also need a critical ear when we hear others trying to quote Scripture. Some proclaim, "God helps those who help themselves," and believe it is a scriptural proverb. You will not find this among the proverbs. The anti-wisdom of the Gospel declares that God helps those who are unable to help themselves, or are willing to help others.

Sometimes we hear there is nothing new with the Gospel or the Church. Preachers can mine the wisdom of Jesus and turn people's lives upside down. The challenge remains: taking an old story and presenting it in a new way, a way that might surprise, shock, or delight our listeners. This demands looking for the hidden nuances in the text, and that often spells the difference between a microwave and a crockpot homily. An example of examining closer the meaning of a text might be the story of the Canaanite woman (Matt 15:21-28). The usual emphasis is on her faith. But a careful exegesis of the text shows that the Matthean emphasis is on bread, and which people have access to bread. Jesus recognized that this woman had already been fed. Is that the reason this story was kept, addressing the problem who has the right to be fed?

Walter Burghardt, s.j., who has studied patristic theology for over six decades, realized that all the wisdom he had accumulated from all these preachers and writers had one purpose: "that I may see more clearly, love more tenderly, and follow more nearly the Wisdom that is Jesus."[5] Are we willing to risk preaching with a similar purpose?

Notes

[1] Keith Russell, "Do Not Confuse Wisdom with Truth," *Living Pulpit* (July–September 2000) 15.

[2] Marcus J. Borg, "The Wisdom of God," *Living Pulpit* (July–September 2000) 7.

[3] Elizabeth A. Johnson, "Images of God's Saving Presence," *Living Pulpit* (July–September 2000) 7.

[4] "Quotations on the Many Views of Wisdom," *Living Pulpit* (July–September 2000) 33.

[5] Walter J. Burghardt, "Jesus, the Wisdom of God," *Living Pulpit* (July–September 2000) 4–5.

Chapter 10

What Did Jesus Preach Most?

When listeners are asked this question, their response is love, compassion, mercy, forgiveness, healing. What Jesus preached most was the reign or kingdom of God. For those interested in statistics you will find some 120 passages dealing with the reign of God, 90 of which are found on the lips of Jesus. Only one reference is found in the Hebrew Scriptures in the book of Wisdom, "She . . . showed him the kingdom of God / and gave him knowledge of holy things" (10:10).

In Mark's Gospel the first words Jesus proclaims are: "This is the time of fulfillment. The kingdom of God is at hand. Repent, and believe in the gospel" (1:15). This is Jesus' inaugural of his preaching, the center of his proclamation, and the theme of Mark's Gospel. Richard McBrien maintains that the reign of God was the main focus of what he did and especially what he said. This message was emphasized not only at meal time (Last Supper), but also throughout his entire ministry. But nowhere does Jesus ever define that the reign of God, which is broader than the church, is the very underpinning of our Christian faith and makes Christians unique. Jesus did use images, parables, healings, and exorcisms to describe or make it come alive. St. Paul refers to God's reign at least fourteen times and wrote that "the kingdom of God is not a matter of food and drink, but of righteousness, peace, and joy in the holy Spirit"

(Rom 14:17). He also said that those who indulge in outbursts of anger, rivalry, jealousy, dissensions, and factions "will not inherit the kingdom of God" (Gal 5:20).

The reign of God is best characterized not by a concept but as a symbol, and in the final analysis is God's unconditional love for us or some deep religious experience. Henri Nouwen describes the reign as creating a community of love. The reign of God is really a person, Jesus Christ. Pope John Paul II in *Redemptoris Missio* writes:

> The Kingdom of God is not a concept, a doctrine or a program subject to free interpretation, but before all else a person with the face and name of Jesus of Nazareth, the image of the invisible God. If the Kingdom is separated from Jesus, it is no longer the Kingdom of God which he revealed.[1]

There are a number of homophones for "reign." It could be spelled "rein" which basically means a discipline, a hold on things, a check that controls. Or it can be spelled "rain" as described by Isaiah:

> For just as from the heavens
>   the rain and snow come down
> And do not return there
>   till they have watered the earth,
>   making it fertile and fruitful . . .
> So shall my word be . . . (55:10-11).

For native Americans there are two kinds of rain. There is a male rain often described as a driving rain coming down in sheets, and a female rain which is a soft, soaking rain. Both are needed to nurture growth. The word "reign" most commonly refers to ruling a certain territory with boundaries. Jesus did not come to establish this kind of reign, which the Jews were expecting from a Messiah. Jesus' reign did not have any boundaries. And because of this position Jesus might have repulsed more people than he attracted. C. S. Lewis once noted that Jesus spoke and acted in such a way that one either had to follow him or else decide that he was crazy (as some did). There was no middle ground in his reign.

Where Is the Reign of God?

Jesus' reign is now, immanent, and in our midst. Jesus said, "The coming of the kingdom of God cannot be observed, and no one will announce, 'Look, here it is,' or, 'There it is.' For behold, the kingdom of God is among you" (Luke 17:20-21). As preachers we make clear to our listeners that this is new in Jesus' proclamation. The time of waiting has come to an end and God's reign has broken into history with Jesus. This reign of God is different. The poor and defenseless in the past were exploited by kings and the ruling classes. This will not be true under God's reign, which will be good news for the poor and helpless.

Preachers have to remind their listeners that God's reign comes alive in them by leading good lives, by being kind, forgiving, and compassionate. This certainly is not the world God intended. A power struggle exists between good and evil. Jesus came to destroy the reign of evil which is still present today. We might not be culpable for the evils in the world like violence, sexism, racism, militarism, but we are still responsible. Culpability usually looks backward whereas responsibility looks forward. We can point our fingers at the many problems facing our country. Some of them cannot be solved, but many can be outgrown or lived more deeply as a mystery. Jung referred to this as a new level of consciousness.

The reign of God will never be fully realized until the Second Coming. It can be compared to an unfinished symphony. We pray in the Our Father, "Your kingdom come." We live in hope that all evil, alienation, hate, egoism, oppression, divisions, pain, death, war will not triumph and that every tear will be wiped away where there will be a new heaven and earth. It can be characterized as the already and not yet, where the last will be first, the oppressed will be free, the hungry and thirsty will be satisfied, and all will be set right. This global and total transformation will be done by the Spirit who continues to create its final form. So we stand precariously on our tiptoes to see what God is birthing among us.

In the meantime we need to challenge our listeners to live in a world filled with sin and tension, which is the difficult part. As we struggle to become more human, using and not burying our talents, ministering to the poor, homeless, hungry, and hopeless, we can invite our listeners to act as a counterculture. We offer them an invitation to realize that all of us are imperfect but are struggling to grow and develop by thinking more of others than ourselves. This invitation can be likened to courtship, which takes place in stages: dates, engagement, and the wedding. The process is slow and laborious, but the results are gratifying and growth-filled.

Images Jesus Used

Jesus used images to convey how the reign of God will come alive. Jesus said:

> The kingdom of heaven is like a mustard seed that a person took and sowed in a field. It is the smallest of all the seeds, yet when full-grown it is the largest of plants. It becomes a large bush, and the "birds of the sky come and dwell in its branches" (Matt 13:31-32).

Actually there is a smaller seed than mustard and we need to point out that the mustard seed does not become a huge and powerful tree like the cedars of Lebanon, which grew to a height of three thousand feet. The redwoods of California are more comparable in size and strength to the cedars of Lebanon. The cedars are described in Ezekiel 17:23; 31:6 and indicate the kind of nation the Israelites had in mind. Jesus said that the reign of God would start out small, but would accomplish as much as some of the most powerful kingdoms. That, indeed, is most consoling.

A theory in physics called the Butterfly Effect maintains that the fluttering of a butterfly wing does have a measured impact throughout the universe. If that is true, we need to impress on our listeners that each one of us can have an impact in our society today. We need not say, "What can I do? I am only one person." Experts point out that using 20 percent of our potential is extraordinary. Anthropologists maintain that we normally use 10 percent of our brain power. If all of this is true, much untapped potential exists within each one of us.

In this reign of God there are no positions of power and success. Values of the true reign of God are stood on their heads. Herod showed his power by killing all the Jewish boys under the age of two. We might ask who the modern-day Herods are. Satan offered Jesus complete political control when he said, "I shall give to you all this power and their glory . . . if you worship me." Jesus said in reply, "It is written: 'You shall worship the Lord, your God, / and him alone shall you serve'" (Luke 4:6-8). And we might ask our listeners, "Whom do we worship, adore? Who is in charge in our lives?"

Yeast

Jesus also said that "the kingdom of heaven is like yeast that a woman took and mixed with three measures of wheat flour until the whole batch was leavened" (Matt 13:33). The author Jeremias believes that three measures of flour would equal fifty pounds. Some three hundred people might be fed from these cakes. Recall that Sarah was told by Abraham when the visitors came, "Quick, three seahs [about a half bushel] of fine flour! Knead it and make rolls" (Gen 18:6).

If a small amount of yeast transforms the dough into bread, our small actions can transform or change a workplace, family, or a community. The transforming power of yeast is slow acting—we cannot see it much like we don't see our fingernails grow. Grace also works quietly and often starts small and accelerates, like the yeast exploding in the dough. If the kneading is done by hand, pounding the dough might offer a good way of releasing tension. Baking was usually a family affair done before the Sabbath. The prophet Jeremiah gave the following picture: "The children gather wood, their fathers light the fire, and the women knead dough to make cakes for the queen of heaven" (7:18). The dough is often lifted into the air and dropped—plop! Why? To remove the air bubbles or imperfections. This might happen to any of our listeners, especially when they experience some trial, difficulty, set back, or loss. But we have to remind them that there is nothing that can compare to a fresh baked loaf of bread. Even the aroma of the baking is pungent.

Jesus also said, "Watch out, guard against the leaven of the Pharisees and the leaven of Herod" (Mark 8:15). This passage follows immediately after the feeding of the five thousand and the Jews asking for a sign. Since leaven was a fermented piece of dough left over from a previous baking, and the Jews considered fermentation evil, they thus considered leaven a symbol of evil. Many Jews deemed leaven comparable to "original sin," which prevents individuals from doing God's will. The Pharisees and Herod considered the reign of God as an earthly reign, based on earthly power won by means of hard fought victories. Jesus did not have this in mind, but the true meaning of God's reign had to evolve.

The apostles also missed the point and were concerned more that they did not bring bread along for the journey. So Jesus gently chided them as a mother does her child at times. Twice before Jesus had satisfied the hungry crowds with food. So he said, "Don't worry. Don't you see how I took care of the people?" Preachers can make different kinds of applications of this passage. Some people are worry-warts and often view life with pessimism or hopelessness. Others, despite their sorrows and disappointments, are hope-filled: their temptations are challenges to be overcome; their sicknesses have some hidden benefit; their insoluble problems become soluble; their breaking points teach them valuable lessons on how to depend more on God.

St. Paul wrote, "A little yeast leavens the whole batch of dough" (Gal 5:9). Here he is pointing out to the Galatians that someone is leading them astray by demanding circumcision and that an individual can be comparable to one bad apple spoiling the whole barrel. Paul is trying to make clear that involvement even with a little evil can corrupt the whole.

Treasure Buried in a Field

Jesus also said, "The kingdom of heaven is like a treasure buried in a field, which a person finds and hides again, and out of joy goes and sells all that he has and buys that field" (Matt 13:44). This passage will undoubtedly sound strange to our listeners but not to the people of Jesus' time. They did not have banks like we do, but stored their cherished belongings in the ground. We can easily recall the man who buried the one talent he received instead of increasing it. Since there were wars and danger of having to move elsewhere, people would bury their precious things in the ground with the hope of retrieving them some day. Years ago some excavators discovered copper pots that were filled with gold, coins of Alexander the Great. You can imagine their joy.

That is the main point of this image that Jesus uses, the joy of discovery. We can imagine the joy our listeners will have once they discover the treasure of God's reign or the pearl of great price. But the key to finding either the treasure or the pearl is the effort needed in searching. Once we have found the treasure or the pearl we can become obsessed about the find. We need to challenge our listeners by asking what they are willing to risk to obtain this treasure or pearl. Are they so taken up with God's reign that they are willing to risk everything? People will laugh at them and consider them fools. But, like St. Paul writes, we become fools for Christ's sake. The key is to risk everything! In giving everything we receive everything, especially joy, and that is the paradox. The rich young man was not willing to risk everything so he went away sad. Real joy is found in risking all that we have. St. Paul came to this realization when he wrote about his relationship to Jesus Christ: "For his sake I have accepted the loss of all things and I consider them so much rubbish, that I may gain Christ" (Phil 3:8).

A threefold basic pattern is found in the images of the treasure or pearl: advent, reversal, and action. The advent takes place when suddenly the individual finds the treasure or pearl. Jesus announces the reign of God as something new and unexpected. The reversal happens when the person has to make a decision: "sells all that he has." Once Jesus proclaims the reign of God, people are challenged to reverse their values and outlook on life. All of this leads or empowers one to action, which is the crucial part and often is lacking in the lives of listeners and maybe in most of our lives.

Image of the Net

Jesus also said that

> the kingdom of heaven is like a net thrown into the sea, which col-
> lects fish of every kind. When it is full they haul it ashore and sit
> down to put what is good into buckets. What is bad they throw
> away. Thus it will be at the end of the age. The angels will go out
> and separate the wicked from the righteous and throw them into
> the fiery furnace, where there will be wailing and grinding of teeth
> (Matt 13:47-50).

Naturally Jesus would use an image of fishing, which could be
done by casting a net into the water or using a drag net, what we
call today trawling. Recall the famous movie "Forrest Gump."
Once Forrest finishes his stint in the army, he and his buddy go
into the fishing business thinking that they will strike it rich. Their
first attempts at catching fish with a net are disheartening. But
they keep on trying and finally are able to succeed.

A drag net will not discriminate what it catches. It will draw in
all kinds of things like weeds, algae, cans, a mixture of fish of all
kinds and sizes. Our listeners need to be reminded that the Church
(which means each one of us) cannot discriminate against anyone.
This is a difficult message to put into practice. Judging who is good
or bad, is not for us to determine. As Jesus points out this will be
done on the final day of judgment. And there will not be an appel-
late court!

Transformed and Commissioned

God's reign is constantly breaking into the world to help
transform it. Sin and evil permeate the world. The various structures of the world need to be subjected to Gospel values so they
become God's reign, not the reign of evil. We have to challenge
our listeners to actively participate in this transformation. Are we
willing to risk this task? This truly is our mission to help create a
loving and harmonious society where peace and justice will pre-
vail. God's reign will always remain God's work and gift, but

everyone can radiate that reign by the way they live and act. We are collaborators in this labor of love until God's reign comes.

Jesus was obsessed with the vision of God's reign. He was willing to work, suffer, die, and rise to make it a reality. He has commissioned us to carry on his ministry. As Diarmuid O'Murchu states in his book *Quantum Theology,* we are invited to labor for a new order in the world where whole and just relationships as well as liberation and peace are found. It does not matter if we are successful. As Mother Teresa of Calcutta once said, it is not important that we are successful but rather that we are faithful. God's reign will be completed when God decides it is time. We are asked to be signs of hope to the hopeless. Hope mobilizes, whereas despair paralyzes. Our mission is to help create a new heaven and a new earth until Jesus comes.

John Fuellenbach, in his book *The Kingdom of God,* writes that

> Jesus himself expressed his mission in these words: "I came to bring fire to the earth and how I wish it were already kindled!" (Luke 12:49). Jesus was drawn by a vision that he compared to "fire." It was definitely not to be understood as a theoretical world view. Jesus' vision aimed at a radical transformation of the world that would upset everything.[2]

He then entrusted this vision to his disciples. We who want to follow in his footsteps will never make this vision acceptable and attractive to anyone if we ourselves are not enthused by it and on fire with it. What the present world seems to be most in need of is people who can provide and radiate an inspiring vision.

Do we as preachers have Jesus' vision of the reign of God, and can we inspire others with his vision?

Notes

[1] John Paul II, *Redemptoris Missio,* On the Permanent Validity of the Church's Mandate, ch. 2, no. 18, December 7, 1990.

[2] John Fuellenbach, *The Kingdom of God* (Maryknoll, N.Y.: Orbis Books, 1995) 3.

Chapter 11

Why Not Preach Paul's Epistles?

During the course of the three cycles the assembly hears significant portions of Paul's writings. Even though the letters are not heard in their entirety, the selections are most impressive. Paul's writings play a significant role in the weekend liturgies. But often these writings are not touched on, as if a stony silence were imposed on them. Many preachers hesitate to comment on these readings and prefer to dwell on the first reading or the gospel. Many reasons can be offered for the silence, but the question remains: Are we willing to risk breaking it?

One reason for silence might be the way the Lectionary has been framed. Priority is given to the first reading, usually from the Old Testament Scriptures, and that reading at times ties in with the gospel. Often there is a link between the first reading and the gospel. The second reading, however, often has little if any connection with the other readings. So what will we preachers choose? If we focus on Paul's readings we necessarily set aside the other readings.

Another difficulty is that Paul's readings are often brief. The gospels in many instances are a story or parable, whereas Paul's writings are usually exhortative or didactic. We can readily preach on the gospel alone because they are better known and recognized. Paul's epistles, however, often require a wider context that needs explanation. Keep in mind that these are letters and were not meant to be heard as segments or snippets. Why Paul even wrote the letter needs to be explained. Preachers have to read the whole letter to better understand Paul's message, and that is time consuming.

Another reason is understanding Paul. As Dr. Richard Lux, who teaches a course on St. Paul at Sacred Heart School of Theology in Hales Corners, points out, we need to remember that Paul is profoundly Jewish. Paul is not a Christian, but a Jew believing that Jesus is the Messiah due to his own experience of the risen Lord. We preachers realize that Paul deals with very difficult topics. Assemblies more readily grasp the gospels than they do Paul's letters. Paul possessed a keen rabbinic mind and wrote in technical language. He presumes that the people he addressed were well versed in the Scriptures (Galatians 2–4). But problems he considered important, like the Mosaic Law, seem irrelevant to us today. Paul was convinced that the Parousia was at hand. His outlook on women is certainly foreign to us. We ask, how does his advice affect us in this second millennium? So it is understandable why we prefer to preach on the first reading or gospel.

Another reason is that modern scholarship attributes the following letters (there are thirteen in all) to Paul: Romans, 1 and 2 Corinthians, Galatians, Philippians, 1 Thessalonians, and Philemon. Most scholars agree that Ephesians, 1 and 2 Timothy, and Titus were written later by other writers. Colossians and 2 Thessalonians are debated by some scholars.

How to Preach Paul

So how are we to preach Paul? We need to keep in mind that the second reading was not intended to be in harmony with the other two readings. If we are going to homilize on Paul's writings, we often have to set aside the other readings unless they can reinforce our main theme or central idea. Above all, the context of Paul's letter needs to be clarified and explained. For example, in 1 Corinthians 12:4-11, Paul speaks of the Spirit's gifts which form a larger portion of the letter elaborating on these gifts, and states we are not to stress the gift of tongues.

In his opening verses to the churches in Corinth—Ephesus and Philippi—Paul addresses them as "holy ones." They certainly had their faults, shortcomings, and sins, especially the Corinthians. Why were they called "holy ones"? Because they were baptized into Christ's Church and had a share in God's divine life. Preachers need to stress this message also, which can be an inspiration for our listeners to deepen their relationship with God and others.

Be aware that Paul's authority in speaking as an apostle was questioned. As author of these letters Paul wrote to address specific problems and situations arising in the various communities. We have to remind ourselves, as Frank Matera insists, not to consider his many writings as theological tracts, or, as some might think, methodical discourses of his theology. He maintains that we should not expect all his theology in any one of his letters. Paul has been described as an "occasional" writer, whenever the situation or occasion demanded it. Daniel Harrington, s.j., advises that once we recognize that Paul is an "occasional" writer, it will prevent us from perusing his writings as theological textbooks. His writings offer encouragement, answer questions, and solve problems.

In reading Paul's letters we often forget that we are receiving Paul's answer, not the question or the problem. It is comparable to listening to only half of a telephone conversation. So we need to ask what occasioned this letter. By carefully reading the letter, and with the help of reliable commentaries, we can ascertain what questions are being asked or problems addressed. This is what we need to explain briefly to our listener. For example, Paul's concern with the Parousia (1 Thess 4:13-18) arose because the Thessalonians were disturbed that the people who already died would not take part in the Parousia. Paul assures them that if Christ has risen from the dead their resurrection is assured and they will take part in the Parousia.

An explanation of the background of the letter is necessary. What prompted Paul to write the letter? What, if any, is the similarity between Paul's congregation and our assembly? Then we can show whatever similarity might be present. The Thessalonians believed that once they died Christ's resurrection was powerless in saving them. Are there people today who feel the same way? It is rather evident how much people put their complete trust in this life. Paul firmly believed that we will be raised because of Christ's resurrection.

Paul wrote with the authority of an apostle (Rom 1:1; Gal 1:1). He saw the Lord (1 Cor 9:1). His letters then carry far more authority. So when these Pauline passages are proclaimed or read it should remind us that Paul is standing in our very midst, for he wrote:

> I, for my part, although absent in body but present in spirit, have already, as if present, pronounced judgment on the one who has committed this deed, in the name of [our] Lord Jesus: when you have gathered together and I am with you in spirit with the power of the Lord Jesus . . . (1 Cor 5:3-4).

In *Paul the Apostle* Christian Beker stresses how Paul's letters need to be interpreted in the light of special incidents which arose in the community. Paul's letters help the Gospel or Good News to come alive and concretize it. His practical advice is ageless.

In 1 Corinthians 11:2-16, Paul dealt with the problems of hairstyles which applied to men and women. We might consider such a passage dated because styles have changed so much over the years. Actually, the passage is concerned more about the Corinthians who believed they had obtained the fullness of salvation, so there were no differences between men and women. Paul was more interested in the eschaton than hairstyles. In God's future reign there will not be male or female, but for now sexual identity was needed.

Paul states, "Any woman who prays or prophecies with her head unveiled brings shame upon her head" (1 Cor 11:5). Remember the days when women had to wear something on their heads in church, even if it was a tissue? At this time some women refused to abide by the customs of having their hair veiled (this was a sign of being married). Paul compared this to wearing short hair connected with prostitutes and with men. He also stated that "women should keep silent in the churches" (1 Cor 14:34), but he already has permitted them to pray and prophecy. This section of Paul deals with spiritual gifts and orderliness concerning their Christian worship. Most likely he was not forbidding formal speech but conversation or idle chatter during the service.

Paul: A Sexist?

Was Paul a sexist? This is a common perception of him. He lived in a male-dominated culture. Scholars point out that the often-quoted passage from Ephesians, "Wives should be subordinate to their husbands" (5:22), actually came from a later disciple of Paul. The passage speaks primarily of Christ's relationship to the Church: "Husbands, love your wives, even as Christ loved the church" (5:25). A closer look at Paul's writings and dealings manifest that he worked intimately with women: Chloe, Prisca and Aquila, Phoebe, Junia, Mary Tryphonea and Tryphosa, Persis, Julia, and others. In Galatians he states that becoming a Christian must change the way we look at one another, "There is neither Jew or Greek, there is neither slave nor free person, there is not male or female; for are all one in Christ Jesus" (3:28). All are equal in God's eyes, and that message must be proclaimed loud and clear.

Diverse cultures existed in Paul's time as they do today. Paul was not only a Jew but a Greek-speaking citizen. Diversity can be found in his letters. He upheld slavery, as is clear in his letter to Philemon. How long did it take the Church to recognize slavery as immoral? How long did it take to allow women to vote? Women play an important role in our society today, providing 85 percent of the services maintaining the Church.

Galatians

If we want to understand Paul's theology, especially the doctrine of justification, we need to examine his letter to the Galatians. Recall that Paul was the first one to preach to them and they were Gentiles. Paul did not demand they be circumcised or even follow the Mosaic Law. Believing in Jesus Christ was sufficient, thus making the Mosaic Law outdated. Paul pictures God as one who wants to save the Gentiles, but there is only so much patience. So there is a limited window of opportunity to save them. Like Abraham bargaining with God for Sodom and Gomorrah, Paul is determined to bring the Gentiles into the scope of salvation. Paul's message was well received like "an angel of God" (4:14). But once Paul left the community, other preachers insisted that circumcision was necessary if they wanted to become Christians. They also attacked Paul's credentials, claiming he was not an authentic apostle. That explains why Paul had to defend himself as well as his preaching.

The problem of circumcision, however, seems so remote to our culture. But there are comparable situations. Living one's faith continues to be a stumbling block for many in our secular society. We live in a society where power, money, success, fame, and fortune are virtues not vices. Do we measure our worth by what we can accomplish or by what we are? To invite listeners to depend more on God contradicts their rugged individualism. Many find it hard to accept what Jesus has done for them. Don't we need something else? Many Galatians were convinced they needed the Mosaic Law. What do we need besides Jesus?

Romans

The letter to the Romans deals with some of the basic themes found in Galatians: the Law, sin, faith, and righteousness. But the audience and situation differ. Instead of a Gentile audience, there is a mixture of Jews and Gentiles, and the problems often arise outside the community. The Gentile Christians are trying to lord it over the Jewish Christians. Does that sound familiar? Paul uses the image of an olive tree to counteract this abuse. The Gentiles were grafted on, the non-Christian Jews were for a time cut off but will be grafted back on (11:13-24). He also contrasts the two groups as sophisticated and scrupulous (14:15). The sophisticated are the Gentile Christians and the scrupulous are the Jewish Christians, a reversal of the Galatian community. So the question arises, how are they to relate to each other with equality and without domination? Paul makes it very clear that both Jew and Gentile have sinned and need God's salvation. But this salvation is revealed in a different way than the Mosaic Law. It is faith in Jesus Christ who frees us from sin, the Law, and death.

The main thrust of the letter concerning the problem of Israel is dealt with in chapters 9–11. Paul asks, "has God rejected his people?" and answers emphatically, "Of course not!" (11:1). John Gager maintains that Paul never says that God had rejected Israel. He also never says that Israel was redeemed through Jesus. Paul argued that God does not change his way of acting. They are still children of Abraham. He points out how they "did not pursue righteousness" (9:30), but their unbelief is short lived. Once the Gentiles are saved then all of Israel is saved. Paul also encouraged the Gentile Christians not to abuse their position of power, but admonished them (Jew and Gentile) to live in harmony and in peace.

The application or relationship to our present age should be evident. The problem of disunity is apparent between Jew and Gentile, Arab and Jew-Palestinians and Israelis, Catholics and Protestants in Ireland, black and white, Anglo and Hispanic, to name a few. All of us are in need of salvation, a better understanding of God's fidelity, and living in harmony with each other. Paul's message could also serve as a reminder for those in authority not to abuse their power.

Corinthians

Paul wrote a number of letters to the Corinthians but we have only two. Even though he founded their community these people were disruptive and not very open to advice. In reading First Corinthians we become aware of all the problems and factions with which Paul had to deal. And you think your parish or community has problems! He found out that a certain man was living with his father's wife, which he described as an "immorality of a kind not found among pagans" (5:1). He advised them on a variety of issues like meat sacrificed to idols, speaking in tongues, the resurrection. But we might ask how are some of these issues pertinent today? We have to remember the deeper issue here is what experts call "realized eschatology." The Corinthians gave the impression that they were already in the eschaton and had achieved full salvation. Paul makes the distinction of the "already" and the "not yet." They were already justified but salvation and its fullness had not yet come.

The Corinthians were so enamored by their charismatic gifts that they believed the eschaton had begun. What else did they need? So they tolerated the case of incest, felt they were immunized from all temptations (7:1-5), could not grasp the danger of idol worship (10:14-22), sensed no need for a future resurrection (15:12), and when they celebrated the Eucharist it was the eschaton lived out.

Paul had to proclaim and remind them of "Christ crucified, a stumbling block to Jews and foolishness to Gentiles" (1:23). The Eucharist was a proclamation of "the death of the Lord until he comes" (11:26). He opposed their glorified or rosy outlook on life with a sound theology of the cross which leads to the resurrected life yet to come. Paul uses the comparison of a seed that dies in order to give a new life to explain what kind of bodily resurrection we will have. Sown corruptible, rises incorruptible; mortal, and rises immortal. In the natural order of things something goes into the ground, and something new is produced.

Our listeners today can also be tricked into believing that there are ways to bypass suffering and the cross. We live in a materialistic world where many are searching for the good life rather than the life that Jesus offers. Our affluent society can give the impression that fullness of salvation has already come. Many other passages dealing with powerlessness, love, hope, death, patience, overconfidence, and courage might be cited to show Paul's relevance today. He was certainly on target and his message lives on.

Harrington believes that Paul's conversations as tent and leather maker may have aided him in spreading Christ's message even more forcefully than when he appeared in a synagogue or a street corner.

How can we follow in Paul's footsteps? It will not be easy because, as we have seen, it demands much effort to read the entire letter and then the particular passage several times. If we do not understand some words, phrases, or sentences, we must consult some reputable commentaries in an effort to obtain the main message of the text. Maybe that will change as we probe deeper into the passage. Finally, decide how to preach this message as forcefully as Paul preached. Paul asks, "How can they hear without someone to preach? And how can people preach unless they are sent? As it is written, 'How beautiful are the feet of those who bring [the] good news!'" (Rom 10:14-15).

Chapter 12

Homilies vs. Eulogies

The Order of Christian Funerals states, "in the face of death, the Church confidently proclaims that God has created each person for eternal life and that Jesus, the Son of God, by his death and resurrection, has broken the chains of sin and death that bound humanity."[1]

This is the challenge and risk that preachers need to keep in mind when preaching on death. We proclaim a God who created us, sent his most precious gift of his son Jesus to save us through his suffering, death, and resurrection. We proclaim a living not a dead God who has given us life in abundance as Jesus said, "I have come that you might have life, and life in abundance" (John 10:10).

The realities of suffering and death present many struggles which we never should take too lightly. Consolation and comfort are important when preaching to the loved ones of the deceased. Hope has to spring eternal as we look beyond this life to a more glorious one. That becomes the essence of the homily as the Order of Christian Funerals encourages the homilist to focus on God's merciful love as well as the paschal mystery.

To accomplish this goal preachers have to make sure their homilies are scripturally based.

> The very meaning and function of the homily is determined by its relation to the liturgical action of which it is a part. It flows from

the Scriptures which are read at that liturgical celebration, or, more broadly, from the Scriptures which undergird its prayers and actions, and it enables the congregation to participate in the celebration with faith.[2]

How often does it happen that funeral homilies make little or no reference to the scriptural readings? The heart of all good preaching is based on God's Word which "speaks" in a forceful manner. Preachers have to show how the personal aspects of the deceased person are clearly connected with the scriptural texts. This can be done by means of a story or an example from the person's life, and often by means of some humor. To find the balance between scriptural proclamations and the person's lived experience is risky and challenging.

Jesus' Presence

One of the ways to console those who have lost a loved one is to ensure them of Jesus' presence in their lives. A cursory glance at Scripture texts, especially the Gospels, makes this abundantly clear. Here, however, there is a need to be specific, not to just say Jesus is present in their lives. A text commonly used is Jesus assuring Martha and Mary, "I am the resurrection and the life" (John 11:25). At the Last Supper Jesus assured his apostles, "Do not let your hearts be troubled. You have faith in God, have faith also in me. In my Father's house there are many dwelling places. . . . I am going to prepare a place for you" (John 14:1-2). When Jesus was ready to ascend into heaven, and knowing that the apostles were fearful, he said, "And behold, I am with you always, until the end of the age" (Matt 28:20). Recently a lady told me how this text which I quoted inspired her to make a commitment to reach out to someone she did not want to help. These and other inspiring passages can assure the bereaved that Jesus is present to help them.

Whatever texts preachers choose will depend on the circumstances of the person's death as well as the needs of the assembly.[3] If it was a sudden death or a prolonged illness, we have to adapt our homily accordingly. A cousin of mine found her husband dead in bed, and she had a very difficult time coping with the shock of his death. When a teenager dies in a car accident it can act as a wake up call for youth who might attend the funeral. When someone has committed suicide we need to help the mourners to grab onto some straws of hope. Maybe Jesus' words to the people concerning Lazarus, "Untie him and let him go," might be appropriate (John 11:44). Our society's view of suicide is often a binding, an exclusion, or a shutting off. Jesus invites us not to bind or shut off but to include. All life is sacred, even that of a convicted murderer. Life is a mystery to be lived not solved. So, rather than expending a lot of psychic energy trying to figure out why something happened, we might encourage the assembly to enter more deeply into the mystery and live it.

Be attuned to the spiritual and psychological conditions of the bereaved. The challenge for the preacher is to make Jesus' presence felt immediately. One way to accomplish this goal might be to use the expression "Jesus says" instead of "Jesus said." In the latter we put Jesus in the past, and in the former we keep Jesus in the present. We need to have Jesus speaking now to grieving people. What a difference when we preach that Jesus *says*, "Come to me, all you who labor and are burdened, and I will give you rest" (Matt 11:28).

Preachers need to ask what emotions surround this occasion. It is apparent that Martha was frustrated and upset when Jesus came only to find that Lazarus was dead. She said, "Lord, if you had been here, my brother would not have died" (John 11:21). We can only imagine the plight of the widow of Naim when her most precious possession, her only son, died. I remember my uncle saying to us that the hardest task in his life was to bury his son, Ralph. We can almost sense Jesus' feelings of loneliness and abandonment in the garden when he said to his apostles, "So you could not keep watch with me for one hour?" (Matt 26:40), or on the cross crying out, "My God, my God, why have your forsaken me?" (Matt 27:46). Preachers are challenged to name the emotion(s) and then help the assembly to reflect on them, especially in relationship to the Scriptures. David Lose believes preaching good homilies at funerals is one of a preacher's most difficult responsibilities, mainly because of the range of emotions present in the people attending the funeral. He maintains that even seasoned preachers are fearful when attempting to comfort and console people filled with intense emotions. We have to place the sorrow of the bereaved into a larger context of Christ's victory over death.

The Power of Scriptural Texts

Scriptural texts have the power to uplift and inspire an assembly. The prophet Isaiah declared:

> [God] will destroy death forever.
> The Lord GOD will wipe away
>   the tears from all faces (25:8).

St. Paul is a master in this area. In rapid fire succession he asks, "What will separate us from the love of Christ?" (Rom 8:35). Absolutely nothing! "If, then, we have died with Christ, we believe that we shall also live with him. We know that Christ, raised from the dead, dies no more; death no longer has power over him" (Rom 6:8-9). "For to me life is Christ, and [therefore] death is gain" (Phil 1:21). In the book of Revelation a voice from heaven is heard, "Write this: Blessed are the dead in the Lord from now on. . . . Let them find rest from their labors, for their works accompany them" (14:13). Or, "He will wipe every tear from their eyes, and there shall be no more death or mourning, wailing or pain, [for] the old order has passed away" (21:4).

We can also quote from poets, writers, and playwrights, like Alfred Lord Tennyson who wrote:

> For tho' from our bourne of time and place
>   The flood may bear me far,
> I hope to see my
>   Pilot face to face
> When I have crossed the bar.[4]

Or Oscar Romero who wrote, "I have often been threatened with death, but as a Christian I do not believe in death without resurrection. If they kill me, I will rise in the Salvadorian people."[5] William Saroyan wrote, probably tongue-in-cheek, "Of course everybody has to die, but I thought an exception would be made in my case."[6] But, meaningful as these or similar passages might be, they will seldom have the impact that scriptural texts possess. As the prophet Isaiah said:

> So shall my word be
>   that goes forth from my mouth;
> It shall not return to me void,
>   but shall do my will
>   achieving the end for which I sent it (55:11).

Before choosing proper texts for the occasion, preachers need to listen attentively to the family or those who are grieving. Detecting their hurts and needs will help us select appropriate passages. Don't inject your own feelings into the situation because they might not be on target. Ask the family to be involved in selecting the scriptural passages, unless they insist on you doing this. Listen closely to what they have to say. One of the touching lines in *Tuesdays with Morrie* is when Morrie Schwartz berates his former student saying softly, "Mitch, you don't understand, I *want* to tell you about my life. I want to tell you before I can't tell you anymore." Whispering he says, "I *want* someone to hear my story. Will you?"[7]

Eulogies

"There is never to be a eulogy" at homily time, the Order of Christian Funerals states.[8] How often those words are disregarded. The word "eulogy" has an interesting derivation; *eu* means "well" and *logus* of course means "word." In Greek it means "good words." A eulogy is an opportunity to speak well of a deceased person, but it must never replace the homily. The major strength of a eulogy is the ability to address the assembly personally. For some preachers it is much easier to eulogize than homilize, and that might be one reason why we hear more eulogies at homily time. We need to remember, however, the role of the homily in the liturgy and the integral part it plays. According to liturgical theologian John Allyn Melloh, a good homily seeks the taproot of the deceased person's life as a Christian, but put in the context of the scriptural passages.

The appropriate time for a eulogy is at a wake or after communion. Some pastors even suggest a certain length of time, and that the eulogy be written out should the person break down while reading it. But a eulogy cannot substitute for a homily. "A homily based on the readings is given at the vigil to help those present find strength and hope in God's saving word."[9] A good homily is also good news proclaiming how Jesus was willing to suffer, die, and rise for us. We celebrate his triumph over death, and also the deceased person who has joined all those marked with the sign of faith now enjoying a life that will never end.

Does this imply we cannot talk about what the person meant to the gathered assembly? The answer is obvious. Pastoral concern would oblige us to be sensitive and compassionate in this area. Even if the deceased showed little interest in the parish or the Church, preachers need to stress God's love, forgiveness, and acceptance. But eulogies are not to be given at homily time.

Eulogies also are not meant to canonize a person. I remember one of our friars who gave a glowing eulogy about his dad at homily time. My response was that he canonized him during homily time. No matter how holy or revered the person, homily time is not the place to put them on a pedestal next to the Blessed Mother or St. Joseph. We can point out or extol their virtues but don't canonize them. We don't need to lie or make up stories either. It reminds me of the story of Bob, who came to a priest and told him about his best friend, Joe, who had just died. Bob said to the priest, "I'll give you $1,000 if you tell the people at his funeral that Joe was a saint." At homily time the priest said, "Joe was an evil man, he lied, cheated on his wife, and got drunk frequently, but next to Bob, he was a saint."

What to Avoid

At times I am called upon to celebrate a funeral Mass for someone whom I did not know. It is not helpful to the family and the assembly to start the homily by stating, "I am sorry, but I did not know him or her." Even when we don't know the deceased person, it is our responsibility, where possible, to learn something about the individual. Listening becomes very crucial. Family members and friends will often tell us some tidbits or anecdotes about the person. Obituaries offer vital information as well. Often these insights can be tied in with the scriptural readings.

Because some preachers have presided at so many funerals their homilies might contain threadbare phrases, pious platitudes, or piffle. Some to avoid are: "Gone but not forgotten," "a diamond in the rough," "we will never see one like him/her again." Theological jargon also weaves its way into some homilies and should be avoided: "God's salvific plan or will," "we will meet him/her in the eschaton." Powerful images are needed to replace these expressions. In the book of Malachi we read, "He will sit refining and purifying [silver], / and he will purify the sons of Levi" (3:3). Scripture scholars wondered why the refiner had to sit. One of the reasons is because the refiner has to remove the dross which rises to the top. After enough dross is removed the refiner is finally able to see his reflection in the silver. This image could be applied to someone who has suffered much during his or her lifetime. Finally, the person perfectly images the Creator and is ready to enter into the glory of God.

Paul expressed the future life well when he wrote:

> What eye has not seen, and the ear has not heard,
> and what has not entered the human heart,
> what God has prepared for those who love him (1 Cor 2:9).

A teacher was giving a graphic description of heaven using many images. At the end she asked the very small children, "How many of you want to go to heaven?" They all raised their hands except little George. "And why don't you want to go to heaven, George," the teacher asked. Looking around at the group, George replied, "Not with this group!"

One tendency among some preachers is telling everything they know about the deceased person. Lengthy eulogies or homilies can easily become boring or cause yawning. Why is there a need to tell all that we know? Another is to tell people how they should feel or to make them cry. One pastor considered his homily a failure if no tears were shed while he preached. The purpose of the homily is an act of praise and thanksgiving to God, especially for having sent Jesus who was willing to suffer, die, and rise for us.

Some Pointers

The Order of Christian Funerals points out three distinct aspects of death: the wake, the funeral Mass, and the committal. They are often referred to as the rite of passage. The vigil service plays an important role, especially if it is used to highlight God's Word, which can console and comfort the bereaved. Maybe more attention needs to be devoted to the committal and its potential. Since cremation is becoming more common, this area also needs further development. In some areas of the country a commemoration of the deceased is made several weeks after the funeral. That enables the shock and numbness to have dissipated, and helps the bereaved to cope better with their loss. Some parishes have a special day set aside, besides All Souls Day, to commemorate all who died during the past year. This is another opportunity to allow God's Word to reflect on Christ's death and resurrection.

David Buttrick once described the brevity of our lives like the hyphen between the dates on our gravestone. How true when compared to eternity. We need to remind our listeners that what matters is not how long we lived, but how well or fully we have lived our hyphen. Jesus lived only thirty-three years, but it was a full life. He said, "I came so that they might have life and have it more abundantly" (John 10:10). Or, another image is the dash between our birth and death. Someone has tried to express it this way: little matter how much we own, the car we drive, the house we live in, or the cash. What really counts is how we have loved others and how we lived the dash.

Preaching at funerals is a privileged occasion and not a burden. People attending these occasions are often of another faith or have not been practicing their Catholic faith. What a marvelous way to evangelize and show the compassion and tenderness shown by Jesus. It is impossible to calculate how many people have been touched deeply by a well-prepared liturgy, homily, and eulogy.

Notes

[1] Order of Christian Funerals (Washington, D.C.: International Commission on English in the Liturgy, 1989) 2.

[2] *Fulfilled in Your Hearing* (Washington, D.C.: United States Catholic Conference, 1982) 17.

[3] Order of Christian Funerals, no. 16, 5.

[4] "Quotations from the Many Views of Death," *Living Pulpit* (July–September 1998) 32.

[5] Ibid., 30.

[6] Ibid.

[7] Mitch Albom, *Tuesdays with Morrie* (New York: Doubleday, 1997) 63.

[8] Order of Christian Funerals, no. 27, 8.

[9] Ibid., no. 61, 24.

Bibliography

Albom, Mitch. *Tuesdays with Morrie*. New York: Doubleday, 1997.

Andrews, Cecile. *The Circle of Simplicity: Return to the Good Life*. New York: Harper Collins, 1997.

Balter, Shlomo. "Helping Ageing Come of Age." *Living Pulpit* (April–June 2000).

Balthasar, Hans Urs von. *A Theological Aesthetics*. New York: Crossroad, 1982.

Beker, Johan Christian. *Paul the Apostle*. Philadelphia: Fortress Press, 1980.

Berry, Thomas. "Imagining Living on the Moon." *National Catholic Reporter* (September 1991).

Bloomer, Nancy. "Preaching to Heal the Earth and to Heal Each Other." *Living Pulpit* (April–June 2000).

Borg, Marcus. *Meeting Jesus Again for the First Time*. San Francisco: HarperSanFrancisco, 1994.

Brown, Rita Mae. *Starting from Scratch*. New York: Bantam Books, 1988.

Brueggemann, Walter. *Finally Comes the Poet*. Minneapolis: Fortress Press, 1989.

Burghardt, Walter J. "To Age Is to Grow." *Living Pulpit* (January–March 2001).

_____. "Jesus, the Wisdom of God." *Living Pulpit* (July–September 2000).

_____. "Just a Church or a Just Church." *Living Pulpit* (October–December 2000).

_____. *Preaching: The Art and Craft.* New York: Paulist Press, 1987.

_____. "Preaching: Twenty-Five Tips." *Church* (Winter 1996).

Burrows, William. "Seeing Sin's Deepest Perversion." *Living Pulpit* (October–December 1999).

Carter, James. *Virtues of Ageing.* New York: Ballantine, 1998.

Case, Patricia. "Talking About Sin, One Expert to Another." *Living Pulpit* (October–December 1999).

Catechism of the Catholic Church. Washington, D.C.: United States Catholic Conference, 1993.

Collingwood, R. G. *The Principles of Art.* Oxford: Clarendon Press, 1938.

Crosby, Michael. "Living Compassionately in a Consumer Culture." *New Theology Review* (May 2000).

D'Arcy, Paula. *Gift of the Red Bird.* New York: Crossroad, 1996.

De Mello, Anthony. *Contact with God.* Chicago: Loyola Press, 1991.

Dethlefsen, Thorwald, and Rudiger Dahlke. *The Healing Power of Illness.* Trans. Peter Lemesurer. Rockport, Mass.: Element, Inc., 1990.

Dyer, Wayne. *There's a Spiritual Solution to Every Problem.* New York: Harper Collins, 2001.

Eliot, T. S. *Four Quartets.* London: Faber & Faber, 1944.

Evangelization in the Modern World. Washington, D.C.: United States Catholic Conference, 1973.

Fox, Matthew. "Celebrating Creation as Blessing." *Living Pulpit* (April–June 2000).

Friedan, Betty. *The Fountain of Age.* New York: Simon and Shuster, 1993.

Fuellenbach, John. *The Kingdom of God.* Maryknoll, N.Y.: Orbis Books, 1995.

Giallanza, Joel. "Spirituality for Religious in Health Care Ministry." *Human Development* (Spring 1994).

Guenther, Margaret. *Toward Holy Ground.* Cambridge, Mass.: Cowley Publications, 1995.

Heilbrun, Caroline. *The Last Gift of Time: Life Beyond Sixty.* New York: Dial Press, 1997.

Hillman, James. *The Force of Character and Lasting Life.* New York: Random House, 1999.

Hopkins, Gerald Manley. "The Blessed Virgin Compared to the Air We Breathe." *The Poems of Gerard Manley Hopkins.* Ed. W. A. Gardner and N. H. MacKenzie. London: Oxford University Press, 1957.

Johnson, Elizabeth. "Images of God's Saving Presence." *Living Pulpit* (July–September 2000).

Kierkegaard, Søren. *Either/Or.* Princeton, N.J.: Princeton University Press, 1971–74.

Knight, David. *Living God's Word.* Cincinnati: St. Anthony Messenger Press, 1999.

Lamott, Anne. *Traveling Mercies.* New York: Pantheon Books, 1999.

Macchia, Frank. "Rediscovering the Church's Charismatic Structure." *Living Pulpit* (October–December 2002).

Manton, Joseph. *The People and the Steeple.* Huntington, Ind.: Our Sunday Visitor Press, 1953.

MacNutt, Francis. *Healing.* Huntington, Ind.: Ave Maria Press, 1974.

McKuen, Rod. *Listen to the Warm.* London: Michael Joseph, 1982.

McMickle, Marvin. "Preaching That Challenges Our Understanding of the Church." *Living Pulpit* (October–December 2002).

_____. "Preaching on Themes in the Creation Story." *Living Pulpit* (April–June 2000).

Morneau, Robert. *Poetry as Prayer: Jessica Powers.* Boston: Pauline Books and Media, 2000.

Ochs, Peter. "Church and Sociality." *Living Pulpit* (October–December 2000).

O'Murchu, Diarmund. *Quantum Theology.* New York: Crossroad, 1997.

Order of Christian Funerals. Washington, D.C.: International Commission on English in the Liturgy, 1989.

Pastoral Statement of Catholic Bishops of Florida. "Companions in Creation." January 1, 1991.

Pierce, Brian. "Sin and Telling the Truth." *Living Pulpit* (October–December 1999).

Pope John Paul II. *Jubilee of the Elderly.* Rome. September 2000.

_____. *Redemptoris Missio.* Encyclical Letter. December 7, 1990.

Pound, Ezra. Letters quoted by Herbert Read. *The True Voice of Feeling: Studies in English Romantic Poetry.* London: Faber & Faber, 1953.

Rahner, Karl. *The Shape of the Church to Come.* New York: Seabury, 1974.

Richards, I. A. *Principles of Literary Criticism.* London: K. Paul, Trench, Trubner, 1938.

Russell, Keith. "Do Not Confuse Wisdom with Truth." *Living Pulpit* (July–September 2000).

Untener, Kenneth. *Preaching Better.* Mahwah, N.J.: Paulist Press, 1999.

Warren, Mervyn. *King Came Preaching.* Downers Grove, Ill.: InterVarsity Press, 2001.

Whitman, Walt. *Leaves of Grass.* New York: Mentor Books, 1954.

Wirzba, Norman. "Noah and the Ark: Becoming Creation." *Living Pulpit* (April–June 2000).